D0688992

ANNE WILLAN'S
LOOK & COOK

Creative Casseroles

ANNE WILLAN'S
LOOK & COOK

Creative Casseroles

DORLING KINDERSLEY
LONDON • NEW YORK • STUTTGART

A DORLING KINDERSLEY BOOK

Created and Produced by
CARROLL & BROWN LIMITED
5 Lonsdale Road
London NW6 6RA

Editorial Director Jeni Wright
Editor Anna Brandenburger
Editorial Assistant Julia Alcock

Managing Art Editor Lyndel Donaldson
Art Editor Lucy De Rosa
Designer Alan Watt
Production Editor Wendy Rogers

First American Edition, 1993
10 9 8 7 6 5 4 3 2 1

Published in the United States by
Dorling Kindersley, Inc., 232 Madison Avenue
New York, New York 10016

Willan, Anne.
    Creative casseroles. – 1st American ed.
      p.   cm. – (Anne Willan's look & cook)
    Includes index.
    ISBN 1-56458-299-X
      1. Casserole cookery.   I. Title.   II. Series: Willan, Anne.
Look & cook.
TX693.W55   1993
641.8'21–dc20   93-3086
                                                       CIP

Reproduced by Colourscan, Singapore
Printed and bound in Italy by A. Mondadori, Verona

CONTENTS

CASSEROLES
THE LOOK & COOK APPROACH

Welcome to **Creative Casseroles** and the *Look & Cook* series. These volumes are designed to be the simplest, most informative cookbooks you'll ever own. They are the closest I can come to sharing my personal techniques for cooking my own favorite recipes without actually being with you in the kitchen looking over your shoulder.

Equipment and ingredients often determine whether or not you can cook a particular dish, so *Look & Cook* sets out everything you need at the beginning of each recipe. You'll see at a glance how long a recipe takes to cook, how many servings it makes, what the finished dish looks like, and how much preparation can be done ahead. When you start to cook, you'll find the preparation and cooking are organized into steps that are easy to follow. Each stage has its own color coding and everything is shown in photographs with brief text to go with each step. You will never be in doubt as to what it is you are doing, why you are doing it, and how it should look.

EQUIPMENT

INGREDIENTS

🍽 SERVES 4–6 　 WORK TIME 25–35 MINUTES 　 COOKING TIME 20–30 MINUTES

I've also included helpful hints and ideas under "Anne Says." These may list an alternative ingredient or piece of equipment, or explain a certain method, or add some advice on mastering a particular technique. Similarly, if there is a crucial stage in a recipe when things can go wrong, I've included some warnings called "Take Care."

Many of the photographs are annotated to pinpoint why certain pieces of equipment work best, and how food should look at the various stages of cooking. Because presentation is so important, a picture of the finished dish with serving suggestions is at the end of each recipe.

Thanks to all this information you can't go wrong. I'll be with you every step of the way. So please come with me into the kitchen to look, cook, and enjoy some **Creative Casseroles**.

WHY CASSEROLES?

A casserole baking in the oven or a hearty stew simmering on the stove is one of the most comforting of home-cooked foods. Often cooked and served in a single pot, casseroles are the solution to today's busy life style where convenience is the key and quick clean-up is mandatory. Casseroles are balanced meals in themselves, combining meat or seafood with nutritious vegetables, and often need no accompaniment except a slice of crusty bread. Whether a slow-cooked country stew or an elegant seafood chowder, there is a casserole for every cook, to suit any occasion.

RECIPE CHOICE

In this book you'll find my favorite casseroles from many countries. Hungary provides the inspiration for *Chicken Paprika with Caraway Dumplings*; *Thai Chicken and Shrimp Stew* adds a flavor of the Far East; while a *garam masala* of cumin, coriander, turmeric, and cayenne pepper gives more than a hint of curry to *Indian Lamb Stew*. New England is the home of *Scallop and Corn Chowder*, while from across the ocean come *Irish Stew* and French *Lamb Chops Champvallon*. There are casseroles with meat, chicken, turkey, or duck, some with fish and shellfish, and some with pasta and vegetables.

SEAFOOD CASSEROLES

Monkfish and White Wine Stew: an elegant recipe, with garden vegetables and white wine. *Monkfish and Red Wine Stew:* red wine adds a robust flavor to this stew of monkfish, mushrooms, and baby onions. *Scallop and Corn Chowder:* the sweetness of scallops and corn is paired with the salt of bacon in this New England classic. *Oyster Stew with Fennel:* the anise flavor of fennel and Pernod highlights the taste of oysters in this sophisticated stew. *Shrimp and Okra Gumbo:* okra gives the characteristic glutinous texture to this gumbo packed with shrimp, oysters, smoked sausage, peppers, and tomatoes. *Gumbo z'Herbes:* spicy mixed greens are mellowed by the addition of a ham hock and sausage in this gumbo. *Paella:* shrimp, mussels, sausage, and chicken are simmered with saffron rice in this quintessentially Spanish dish. *Seafood Paella:* invite family or friends to enjoy this rice dish of squid, shrimp, and clams. *Five-Spice Fillet of Salmon:* salmon, with the exotic flavor of Chinese five-spice powder, is pan-fried then baked on a bed of carrots, zucchini, and leeks. *Salmon Fillets with Mushroom and Leek Julienne:* an elegant dish of pink salmon with contrasting julienne of mushrooms and leeks. *Seafood and Tomato Stew:* a hearty stew of fragrant tomato broth packed with crabs, mussels, scallops, and white fish. *Fish Cioppino:* a variety of fish, including halibut, monkfish, and tuna, are simmered in this delicious stew.

POULTRY AND MEAT CASSEROLES

Chicken Paprika with Caraway Dumplings: from eastern Europe, this rich stew is flavored with paprika and dotted with caraway dumplings. *Chicken and Paprika Pilaf:* rice and chicken are cooked with tomatoes, green bell pepper, onion, garlic, paprika, and oregano. *Chicken and Beer Stew:* chicken takes on a robust flavor, cooked in dark beer with juniper berries and onions. *Chicken with Cognac:* for a sophisticated dinner, chicken is simmered with baby onions and Cognac. *Chicken in a Pot:* a whole chicken is poached in chicken broth, with aromatic vegetables, then served with sauce gribiche for a two-course meal. *Tarragon Chicken:* a classic dish of chicken in a rich tarragon-cream sauce with turnips. *Turkey Mole:* in this simplified recipe of a Mexican dish, chili powder adds heat to the rich, aromatic sauce with unsweetened chocolate. *Pork Mole:* pork chops are cooked in a spicy sauce and served with sour cream. *Baby Chickens with Plums and Cabbage:* small whole birds are cooked *en cocotte* with shredded cabbage, bacon, and purple plums for a touch of sweetness. *Baby Chickens with Carrots and Cabbage:* a light but satisfying country-style casserole that is ideal for winter days. *Malaysian Chicken and Shrimp Stew:* bean sprouts, coconut milk, tofu, ginger, fresh coriander (cilantro), and spices give an Asian twist to chicken and shrimp; thin rice noodles thicken the stew. *Thai Chicken and Shrimp Stew:* fresh hot chili peppers and lemon grass make the Thai version of chicken and shrimp. *Duck with Turnips and Apricots:* duck is cut up and cooked with turnips, dried apricots, and Madeira wine for a touch of sweetness. *Duck with Fresh Figs and Port Wine:* fresh figs contrast with the richness of duck in a port wine sauce. *Indian Lamb Stew:* slow cooking imparts mellow flavor to lamb, with lentils, eggplant, and cauliflower in a spicy sauce. *Indian Chicken Stew:* chicken replaces the lamb, while chickpeas add body to this spicy stew. *Lamb Chops Champvallon:* this French dish of lamb chops baked between slices of potato and onion dates back from the time of Louis XIV. *Irish Stew:* leeks take the place of onions for a contemporary update on the famous family dish. *Baked Ham and Prunes in Rich Wine Sauce:* ham is baked with prunes in a sweet-sour sauce with vinegar and caramel. *Ham with White Wine and Apples:* white wine, cream, and apples add succulence to thick slices of ham. *Beef, Barley, and Mushroom Stew:* barley adds body and character to beef and mushrooms simmered in beef stock. *Barley and Vegetable Stew:* in this stew, green peas, corn, carrots, celery, and onions are cooked with barley. *Portuguese Pork and Clam Stew:* clams add zest to tender pork marinated in white wine flavored with herbs, then slowly cooked with onions and tomatoes. *Chilean Pork and Beans:* a hearty pork stew packed with beans, bell peppers, tomatoes, potatoes, and herbs. *French Beef and Herb Potato Pie:* ground beef acquires French chic when combined with white wine, tomatoes, and garlic, then topped with a layer of creamy potato purée flavored with basil and parsley. *Old Emily's Shepherd's Pie:* ground lamb is the base for this family favorite, baked in

individual dishes. *Peppery Tuscan Beef Stew:* sage-flavored *fettunta* (toasts) accompany this rustic Italian stew of beef, tomatoes, pancetta, red wine, and garlic, with plenty of black pepper for piquancy. *Italian Beef and Rosemary Stew:* typical Italian ingredients, rosemary and olives, marry with beef and a dry white wine for a warming winter treat. *Springtime Veal Stew:* fresh fennel adds flavor and carrots give color to the pale delicacy of veal in an ivory cream sauce that is thickened with egg yolk. *French White Veal Stew:* a classic white *blanquette* of button mushrooms and veal in a rich cream sauce. *Mock Venison Stew:* lamb shanks are transformed to resemble venison by marinating and braising in red wine with aromatic vegetables. *Venison Stew with Pears:* wedges of pear show how successful the partnership of fruit with game can be.

VEGETABLE AND PASTA CASSEROLES

Perfect Pasta and Cheese: quill-shaped pasta baked in a rich cheese sauce, embellished with both wild and common mushrooms, makes a sophisticated version of macaroni and cheese. *Perfect Pasta with Three Cheeses:* green spinach pasta gives flavor and color contrast to the rich sauce of the hard, blue-veined, and creamy French cheeses. *Bell Pepper and Mushroom Lasagne:* plenty of roasted red and green bell peppers, with mushrooms, tomato sauce, and ricotta cheese make a light and tasty lasagne. *Lasagne with Spinach:* an attractive supper dish of layers of green spinach, red tomato sauce, and white ricotta cheese– the colors of the Italian flag. *Eggplant Parmigiana:* the classic of sliced eggplant

layered with a rich tomato sauce, basil, mozzarella, and freshly grated Parmesan cheese – topped with more cheese then baked until bubbling and brown. *Tian of Mediterranean Vegetables:* eggplant and zucchini slices, baked with tomatoes, onions, and thyme, go into my version of a Provençal *tian*, or baked vegetable dish.

EQUIPMENT

The range of dishes is wide in this book, but the equipment needed to make them is very simple. Basic, of course, is the casserole dish itself. It should have a tight-fitting lid with a heatproof handle, though you can cover it with a double layer of foil. Enameled cast iron is a favorite because it spreads the heat evenly and looks attractive. Other materials include stainless steel, which is easy to keep clean, but should have an aluminum or copper base, and anodyzed aluminum which is light in weight and spreads heat well. The Dutch oven is excellent for cooking but must be kept oiled to prevent it from rusting in humid air.

You will also need a baking dish; the size will be stated in the recipe. You have the option of heatproof glass, porcelain, and earthenware. Enameled cast iron gratin dishes can also be used. Note that metal takes time to heat in the oven, so baking time may be approximate.

You will need a chef's knife for cutting up poultry and meat and for preparing large vegetables, plus a small knife for small to medium vegetables. Knives should be regularly sharpened and stored carefully so the edges remain sharp. Never soak knives or put them in the dishwasher.

In many recipes, a 2-pronged fork is used with meat and poultry during and after frying. Some recipes call for a food processor or blender, for instance to purée the sauce mixture for Turkey Mole. Others require a potato masher or ricer to make the potato purée topping.

If you are preparing a recipe that involves marinating meat, poultry, fish, or vegetables, use a non-metallic bowl so it will not react with the acid in the marinade.

INGREDIENTS

Starting with the main ingredients, seafood lovers can choose from casseroles with shrimp, mussels, oysters, and scallops, or fish such as monkfish, salmon, halibut, and cod. Poultry includes a chicken simmered with vegetables, chicken pieces in a variety of tempting sauces, plus recipes for duck with fruit, and turkey in a Mexican mole sauce.

The four main meats – beef, lamb, pork, and veal – feature frequently. Often less expensive cuts can be used in a casserole, as the long slow cooking tenderizes them. When combined with hearty grains and pulses, such as barley, dried beans, and lentils, you can create a substantial meal to feed the whole family. A handful of recipes are based on pasta, including some vegetarian ideas.

Stocks – beef, veal, chicken, or fish – can be the backbone of a casserole, intensifying the flavors while providing liquid in which to cook the ingredients. Equally important is the allium family – onions, garlic, and shallots, while earthy roots such as potatoes, turnips, leeks, and carrots add substance. Leafy greens, cabbage, okra, corn, and fennel all appear in these casserole recipes. Both wild and common mushrooms play a role, as do the sun-loving vines: eggplant, tomatoes, bell peppers, and squash. Fruit is teamed with meat and poultry to add a touch of sweetness, while dried and fresh chili peppers, fresh ginger root, coconut milk, lemon grass, vinegar, and lemon juice add a further dimension, together with spices such as cayenne, nutmeg, cinnamon, cumin, and turmeric. You'll also find familiar fresh herbs. Their fragrant leaves are either added at the beginning of cooking to blend with other ingredients or are stirred into a casserole at the last minute to impart fresh flavor and color.

TECHNIQUES

You'll be shown many useful techniques in this book, because casseroles are so diverse. The preparation of everyday vegetables is covered: peeling, seeding, and chopping tomatoes; slicing and chopping onions, bell peppers, carrots, leeks, and potatoes; and shredding cabbage. You will see how to peel bell peppers by roasting them first, which also gives them a delicious smoky flavor. Peeling and crushing garlic is made simple with a quick blow from a heavy knife-blade. None of these techniques is difficult, and you will soon master the common ones.

In addition, you will learn how to carry out tasks as varied as trussing and cutting up a chicken. There are instructions on preparing fresh ginger root by peeling, crushing, and chopping it. Cleaning and cooking mussels is explained, as well as removing the vein from shrimp.

Cooking techniques are varied. Sometimes meat or poultry are browned before being simmered in a liquid, to add flavor and color. In other recipes meat is added raw to a liquid, then cooked very gently for a long time, to soften and add richness to the sauce.

Many casseroles include a sauce. I show you how to make a cheese sauce and a rich brown roux (flour and oil mixture) to give the characteristic flavor to a Louisiana gumbo. Some sauces are lightly thickened with arrowroot. Reduction of cooking liquid is the key to good sauces, and you'll find this clearly explained too.

MONKFISH AND WHITE WINE STEW

🍽️ SERVES 6   🥣 WORK TIME 45–50 MINUTES   ♨️ COOKING TIME 25–30 MINUTES

EQUIPMENT

colander

large frying pan

chef's knife   paper towels

small knife   metal spatula

saucepans, 1 with lid

bread knife

wooden spoon

chopping board

The delicate flavor of monkfish is highlighted with fresh vegetables and white wine. Kneaded butter thickens the sauce to a velvety consistency.

GETTING AHEAD

The vegetable broth can be cooked up to 8 hours ahead and kept, covered, in the refrigerator. Reheat it gently on top of the stove, then cook the fish, and finish the stew.

SHOPPING LIST

1¹/₂ lb	skinned monkfish fillets
	salt and pepper
2	shallots
2	garlic cloves
2	leeks
¹/₂ lb	mushrooms
1	small bunch of parsley
3–5	sprigs of fresh thyme
1 lb	small zucchini
5 tbsp	butter, at room temperature
1	bay leaf
1 cup	dry white wine
2 cups	fish stock (see box, page 124)
3 tbsp	flour
	For the fried croûtes
6	slices of white bread
3 tbsp	butter
3 tbsp	vegetable oil

INGREDIENTS

fish stock

parsley

leeks

white bread

monkfish fillets

vegetable oil   butter

shallots

zucchini

bay leaf

flour

garlic

mushrooms

thyme   dry white wine

ORDER OF WORK

1 PREPARE THE MONKFISH AND THE VEGETABLES

2 SIMMER THE BROTH; MAKE THE CROUTES

3 COOK THE FISH AND THICKEN THE STEW

1 PREPARE THE MONKFISH AND THE VEGETABLES

Membrane on monkfish
must always be completely
removed

1 If necessary, cut away the
thin membrane that covers the
monkfish. Rinse the fish in cold water
and pat dry with paper towels. Holding
each fillet steady, cut diagonal slices
about ½-inch thick using the chef's
knife. Season with salt and pepper.

2 Peel the shallots; separate them
into sections, if necessary. Slice
each one horizontally, then vertically,
toward the root, leaving the slices
attached. Cut across into dice. Lightly
crush each garlic clove. Discard the
skin and finely chop the garlic.

3 Trim the leeks. With the
chef's knife, slit them
lengthwise, then cut
them diagonally into
½-inch pieces.

Slit leeks before washing
to open out layers

4 Wash the leeks thoroughly in the
colander, under cold running
water. Leave them to drain well.

5 Wipe the mushroom caps with
damp paper towels and trim the
stems even with the caps. Cut the
mushrooms into quarters.

7 Trim the zucchini and cut them
into 2-inch pieces. Cut each piece
lengthwise into quarters. With the
small knife, cut away the seeds
and trim the edges of the pieces
to give a rounder shape.

Zucchini pieces
will form neat
shapes for stew

Zucchini are trimmed
into torpedo-shaped
pieces

6 Strip the parsley and thyme leaves
from the stems. Pile the parsley
leaves on the chopping board and
finely chop them with the chef's knife.

2 SIMMER THE BROTH; MAKE THE CROUTES

1 Melt 2 tbsp of the butter in a large saucepan, sauté the shallots, garlic, and leeks, stirring occasionally, until soft, 3–5 minutes.

Leeks, garlic, and shallots are softened in butter to mellow flavor

2 Add the mushroom quarters, thyme, bay leaf, salt, and pepper to the saucepan, and stir to combine. Pour in the white wine and fish stock, cover the saucepan with the lid, and simmer, 10–15 minutes.

3 Add the zucchini and continue cooking until the vegetables are just tender, 8–10 minutes longer.

4 Meanwhile, cut the crusts from the bread, then cut each slice into 4 triangles. Melt one-third of the butter and oil in the frying pan. Add 8 bread triangles and fry until golden, 1–2 minutes. Turn the croûtes, and continue frying until golden, 30–60 seconds longer. Drain on paper towels and fry the remaining croûtes in the remaining butter and oil in 2 batches.

Fried croûtes are easily turned using metal spatula

Triangular croûtes will brown evenly when fried in batches

ANNE SAYS
"The croûtes can be prepared ahead. Wrap them in foil so they are easy to reheat in a low oven."

3 COOK THE FISH AND THICKEN THE STEW

1 Add the monkfish to the broth with water, if necessary, so that the fish is barely covered, and stir to combine.

! TAKE CARE !
Stir the stew gently so the monkfish does not fall apart.

2 Cover the pan, bring back to a boil, and simmer until the fish is tender when tested with a fork, 3–5 minutes.

3 Make the kneaded butter: using a fork, blend the remaining 3 tbsp butter with the flour to form a smooth paste. Add to the boiling broth. Stir to combine, so the butter melts and the flour thickens the stew. Simmer, 2 minutes.

Stir kneaded butter gradually into stew so it melts evenly

4 Discard the bay leaf, stir in half of the chopped parsley, and taste the stew for seasoning.

🍴 TO SERVE
Transfer the stew to a warmed tureen, sprinkle with the remaining parsley, and serve with the fried croûtes.

Monkfish retains firm texture in hearty stew

Crunchy croûtes are good contrast to velvety stew

V A R I A T I O N

MONKFISH AND RED WINE STEW

Known in French as Lotte en Meurette, *this dish commonly includes mushrooms and baby onions in the sauce.*

1 Omit the garlic, leeks, parsley, thyme, zucchini, and white wine. Prepare the monkfish, shallots, and mushrooms as directed.
2 Make the croûtes as directed. Cook the shallots in 2 tbsp butter until soft, 1 minute. Add 2 cups red wine and simmer until reduced by half.
3 Meanwhile, peel ½ lb baby onions. Melt 2 tbsp butter in a frying pan, add the onions and cook until golden, 5–8 minutes. Add the mushrooms, and cook until the liquid evaporates and the mushrooms are tender, 3–5 minutes.
4 Add 2 cups fish stock and 1 bay leaf to the red wine. Add the monkfish and cover. Return to a boil and simmer until the fish is tender, 3–5 minutes.
5 Stir in the onions and mushrooms and thicken the stew as directed with the kneaded butter. Serve on warmed individual plates.

SCALLOP AND CORN CHOWDER

🍽 SERVES 6–8 🥄 WORK TIME 25–30 MINUTES 🍲 COOKING TIME 15–20 MINUTES

EQUIPMENT

large pot

colander

chopping board

paper towels

bowls

wooden spoon

slotted spoon

chef's knife

small knife

vegetable peeler

INGREDIENTS

onions

bay leaf

paprika

fresh corn †

bacon

light cream

fish stock ‡

scallops

new potatoes

milk

† 2 cups defrosted corn kernels can also be used

‡ half bottled clam juice, half water can also be used

ANNE SAYS
"For a lighter chowder, you can substitute milk for the cream."

This New England classic marries the sweetness of scallops and corn with the salt of bacon, adding potatoes for body. You can use either bay or sea scallops. Oyster crackers are the traditional accompaniment.

GETTING AHEAD

The chowder can be prepared, without the scallops, up to 1 day ahead and kept, covered, in the refrigerator. Gently reheat it on top of the stove until simmering, and cook the scallops just before serving.

SHOPPING LIST

½ lb	bacon slices
2	medium onions
4	ears of fresh corn
1 lb	red-skinned new potatoes
1½ lb	bay or sea scallops
1	bay leaf
	salt and pepper
3 cups	fish stock (see box, page 124)
1 cup	light cream
2 cups	milk
	paprika for sprinkling

ORDER OF WORK

1 PREPARE THE CHOWDER INGREDIENTS

2 COOK THE CHOWDER

1 PREPARE THE CHOWDER INGREDIENTS

1 Stack the bacon slices on the chopping board and cut them crosswise into strips about 1/2-inch wide, using the chef's knife.

Stacking bacon slices makes cutting into strips quicker

2 Peel the onions with the small knife, leaving a little of the root attached. Halve and thinly slice the onions (see box, below).

3 Hold each ear of fresh corn vertically on the chopping board, and cut from the tip down to the board with the chef's knife. Rotate the ear, and continue removing as many kernels as possible. Put the kernels in a small bowl. Working over the bowl, with the back of the knife, scrape all the pulp and milk from each ear of corn.

Corn adds sweetness to chowder

Back of knife is best for pressing pulp from ears of corn

HOW TO SLICE AN ONION

Onions are often sliced for soups and stews, as well as for sautéing. The root is left on for slicing, to help hold the onion together.

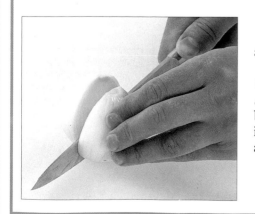

1 Using a chef's knife, cut the onion lengthwise in half through the root and stem end.

2 Lay each half, cut-side down, on a chopping board, and cut across into thin or thick slices, as required.

Cut onion into slices of even thickness

4 Peel the potatoes, using the vegetable peeler. With the chef's knife, cut each potato into 4–5 pieces, depending on its size.

5 If necessary, discard the tough, crescent-shaped membrane at the side of each scallop. Rinse the scallops in a bowl of cold water, and drain. If using large sea scallops, cut each one into 2 rounds.

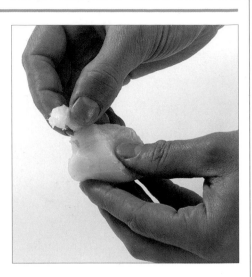

2 COOK THE CHOWDER

1 Heat the large pot, add the bacon, and fry, stirring with the wooden spoon, until the fat is rendered (melted), 3–5 minutes. With the slotted spoon, transfer the bacon to a plate lined with paper towels.

2 Lower the heat, then add the sliced onions, and cook, stirring frequently with the wooden spoon, until soft and translucent, 3–5 minutes. With the slotted spoon, transfer the onions to the lined plate. Discard any remaining fat from the pot.

Pour in fish stock to cover potatoes generously

3 Add the potatoes to the pot with the bay leaf, salt, and pepper. Pour in the fish stock. Bring to a boil and simmer gently until the potatoes are just slightly soft when pierced with the tip of the small knife, 7–10 minutes.

After stock has been added, stir to dissolve browned juices at bottom of pot

4 Return the cooked bacon and onions to the pot with the corn kernels and their pulp; stir to combine.

5 Pour in the cream and milk, and stir until blended. Bring to a boil and simmer until the potatoes are tender, 7–10 minutes longer.

6 Add the scallops to the pot, and stir to combine. Bring the chowder just back to simmering, then remove the pot from the heat. Discard the bay leaf, taste the chowder for seasoning, and adjust if needed.

! TAKE CARE !
Do not overcook the scallops or they will be tough; the heat of the chowder will continue to cook them after the pot is removed from the heat.

⊕ TO SERVE
Serve the chowder in bowls, sprinkled with paprika. Accompany with oyster crackers, if you like.

Bacon contrasts with sweetness of scallops and corn

VARIATION

OYSTER STEW WITH FENNEL

In this southern stew, oysters are paired with fennel and a dash of Pernod.

1 Omit the onions, corn, and fish stock. Substitute 32 fresh or bottled oysters (about 1 pint), for the scallops, reserving the oyster juice.

2 Chop the bacon and prepare the potatoes as directed. Trim and slice 2 large fennel bulbs (total weight about 1½ lb). Strain the oyster juice into a measuring cup and add enough water to make 3 cups liquid.

3 Fry the bacon as directed until crisp, and remove it from the pot. Add the sliced fennel and cook gently, stirring occasionally, until very soft and just starting to brown, 15–20 minutes.

4 Add the potatoes, bay leaf, salt, and pepper to the pot and pour over the oyster liquid. Bring to a boil and simmer until the potatoes begin to soften, 7–10 minutes.

5 Add half of the bacon, the cream, and milk; simmer until the potatoes are tender, 7–10 minutes longer.

6 Stir in the oysters and simmer just until their edges curl, 30–60 seconds. Remove the stew from the heat, stir in 3–4 tbsp Pernod or other anise liqueur, and taste for seasoning. Spoon the stew into 6–8 warmed individual bowls, and sprinkle with the reserved bacon.

SHRIMP AND OKRA GUMBO

¶O¶ SERVES 8   ◑ WORK TIME 45–50 MINUTES*   ♨ COOKING TIME 1–1¼ HOURS

EQUIPMENT

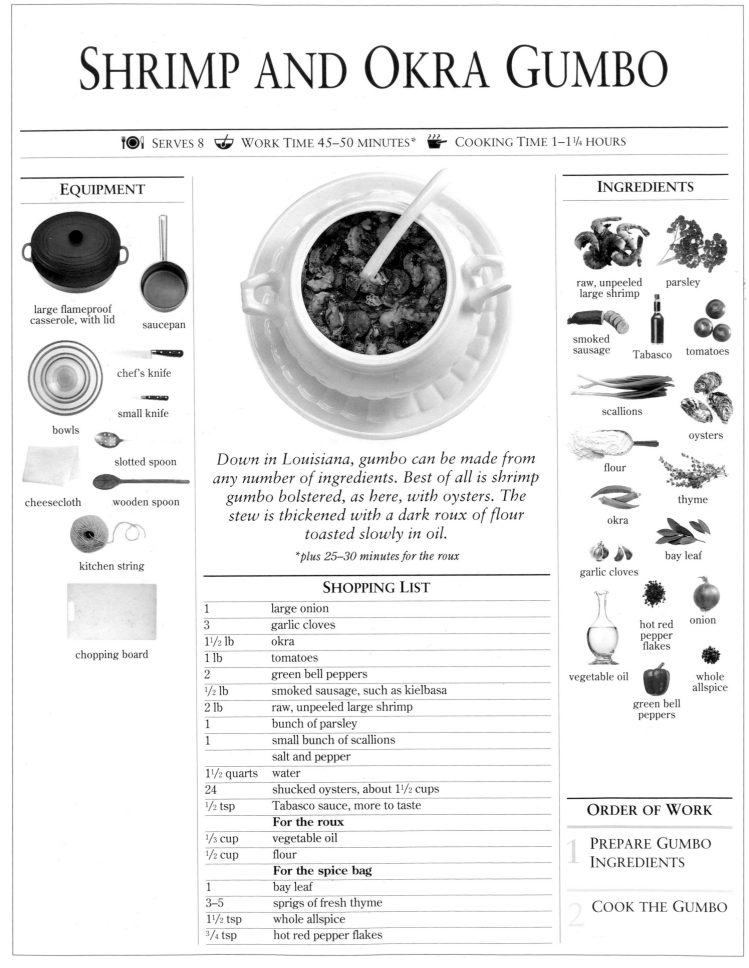

large flameproof
casserole, with lid

saucepan

chef's knife

small knife

bowls

slotted spoon

cheesecloth

wooden spoon

kitchen string

chopping board

*Down in Louisiana, gumbo can be made from
any number of ingredients. Best of all is shrimp
gumbo bolstered, as here, with oysters. The
stew is thickened with a dark roux of flour
toasted slowly in oil.*

plus 25–30 minutes for the roux

INGREDIENTS

raw, unpeeled
large shrimp

parsley

smoked
sausage

Tabasco

tomatoes

scallions

oysters

flour

thyme

okra

bay leaf

garlic cloves

vegetable oil

hot red
pepper
flakes

onion

green bell
peppers

whole
allspice

SHOPPING LIST

1	large onion
3	garlic cloves
1½ lb	okra
1 lb	tomatoes
2	green bell peppers
½ lb	smoked sausage, such as kielbasa
2 lb	raw, unpeeled large shrimp
1	bunch of parsley
1	small bunch of scallions
	salt and pepper
1½ quarts	water
24	shucked oysters, about 1½ cups
½ tsp	Tabasco sauce, more to taste
	For the roux
⅓ cup	vegetable oil
½ cup	flour
	For the spice bag
1	bay leaf
3–5	sprigs of fresh thyme
1½ tsp	whole allspice
¾ tsp	hot red pepper flakes

ORDER OF WORK

1 PREPARE GUMBO
INGREDIENTS

2 COOK THE GUMBO

1 PREPARE GUMBO INGREDIENTS

1 Peel the onion, leaving a little of the root attached; cut it lengthwise in half. Slice each half horizontally, then vertically, toward the root, leaving the slices attached at the root end. Finally, cut across to make dice.

2 Set the flat side of the chef's knife on top of each garlic clove and strike it with your fist. Discard the skin and finely chop the garlic.

Okra will give characteristic slightly glutinous texture to gumbo

3 With the chef's knife, trim the stems and tips from the okra; cut the okra crosswise into ³⁄₈-inch slices.

Neatly cut pieces ensure okra will cook evenly

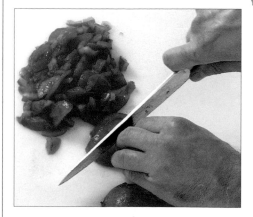

4 Cut the cores from the tomatoes and score an "x" on the base of each. Immerse in boiling water until the skins start to split, 8–15 seconds, depending on their ripeness. Transfer at once to a bowl of cold water. When cool, peel off the skins. Cut them crosswise in half, squeeze out the seeds, then coarsely chop each half.

HOW TO PEEL AND DEVEIN SHRIMP

Shrimp have a dark intestinal vein along the back that should be removed before cooking.

Shell comes off easily in your fingers

1 Peel all of the shell from each shrimp with your fingers, and discard the shell.

2 Using a small knife, make a shallow cut along the back of the shrimp.

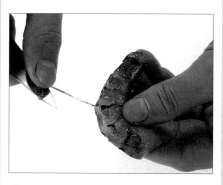

3 With the help of the small knife, gently pull out the dark intestinal vein and discard it.

5 Core the bell peppers. Halve them and scrape out the seeds. Slice lengthwise into thin strips. Gather the strips together and cut into dice.

6 If necessary, remove the outer casing from the sausage. Using the chef's knife, cut the sausage into 1/4-inch slices. Peel and devein the shrimp (see box, page 19).

7 Make the spice bag: combine the bay leaf, thyme, allspice, and hot red pepper flakes; tie them up in a piece of cheesecloth.

Cheesecloth lets out flavor but holds in spices

8 Strip the parsley leaves from the stems, and finely chop the leaves. Trim the roots and tough green tops from the scallions. Slice them crosswise on the diagonal, including some of their green tops.

2 COOK THE GUMBO

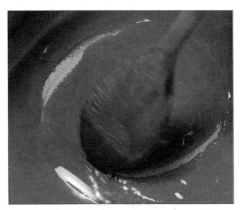

1 Make the roux: heat the oil in the casserole. Stir in the flour and cook over very low heat, stirring constantly with the wooden spoon, until the roux is medium brown, 25–30 minutes.

ANNE SAYS

"To avoid constant stirring, cook the roux in a 450°F oven for the same time. When thoroughly cooked, the roux should be a dark caramel color."

2 Stir the onions, garlic, bell peppers, salt, and pepper into the roux, and cook, stirring constantly, until they are softened and just lightly browned, 7–10 minutes. Add the tomatoes and sausage to the casserole and stir to combine. Cook, stirring occasionally, 10–12 minutes longer.

3 Add the okra, spice bag, and water. Partially cover the casserole and simmer, stirring occasionally, until the okra is very tender and the gumbo is thick and rich, 40–50 minutes.

4 Just before serving, add the prepared shrimp to the gumbo and simmer gently until they begin to lose their transparency and start to turn pink, 3–5 minutes.

5 Stir in the oysters and scallions; cook until the edges of the oysters start to curl, 1–2 minutes longer.

! TAKE CARE !
Do not overcook the oysters or they will be tough and chewy.

6 Remove from the heat and discard the spice bag. Stir in the chopped parsley and Tabasco sauce. Taste for seasoning, adding more Tabasco sauce, if you like.

Hot Tabasco sauce is usual way to spice gumbo

🍽 TO SERVE
Spoon the gumbo into a warmed tureen or into individual soup bowls. Serve very hot.

Shellfish and smoked sausage is a popular Louisiana combination

VARIATION

GUMBO Z'HERBES

This gumbo is usually made with a variety of greens. Tradition has it that you invite as many friends as the number of greens you serve.

1 Omit the tomatoes, bell peppers, parsley, scallions, shrimp, and oysters. Slice the sausage and okra as directed.
2 Wash the leaves from ³/₄ lb each of collard and mustard greens, watercress, and 1 head of escarole (about ³/₄ lb), discarding any tough stems.
3 Put the wet greens in a large casserole and sprinkle with salt. Cover, and steam, stirring frequently, 10–12 minutes. Drain the greens; reserve any cooking liquid. Let them cool, then roughly chop them .
4 Make the spice bag as directed, adding 3–5 sprigs of fresh oregano.
5 Make the roux; cook the onions and garlic as directed. Stir in the chopped greens, 1 meaty smoked ham hock (about 1 lb), the sausage, okra, water, and cooking liquid from the greens.
6 Cover and simmer until the greens are very tender and the meat falls easily from the ham hock, 1¹/₄–1¹/₂ hours. Pull off the meat, shred it, and stir it back into the greens. Taste the gumbo and serve it over boiled rice.

GETTING AHEAD

The gumbo can be prepared, without the shrimp and oysters, 1–2 days ahead and kept, covered, in the refrigerator – the okra will make it thicken on standing. Gently reheat, adding more water if it is too thick. Add the shrimp and oysters just before serving.

PAELLA

🍽 SERVES 8–10   🥣 WORK TIME 1 HOUR   ♨ COOKING TIME 40–45 MINUTES

EQUIPMENT

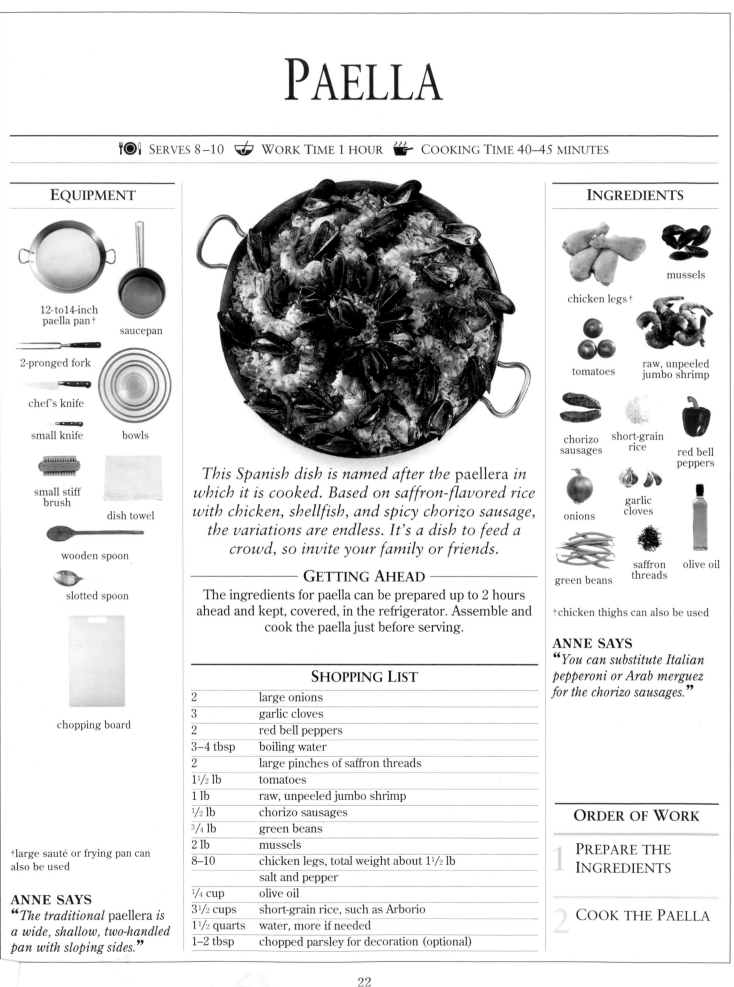

12-to14-inch paella pan †

saucepan

2-pronged fork

chef's knife

small knife

bowls

small stiff brush

dish towel

wooden spoon

slotted spoon

chopping board

†large sauté or frying pan can also be used

ANNE SAYS
"The traditional paellera is a wide, shallow, two-handled pan with sloping sides."

INGREDIENTS

chicken legs †

mussels

tomatoes

raw, unpeeled jumbo shrimp

chorizo sausages

short-grain rice

red bell peppers

onions

garlic cloves

green beans

saffron threads

olive oil

†chicken thighs can also be used

ANNE SAYS
"You can substitute Italian pepperoni or Arab merguez for the chorizo sausages."

This Spanish dish is named after the paellera *in which it is cooked. Based on saffron-flavored rice with chicken, shellfish, and spicy chorizo sausage, the variations are endless. It's a dish to feed a crowd, so invite your family or friends.*

GETTING AHEAD

The ingredients for paella can be prepared up to 2 hours ahead and kept, covered, in the refrigerator. Assemble and cook the paella just before serving.

SHOPPING LIST

2	large onions
3	garlic cloves
2	red bell peppers
3–4 tbsp	boiling water
2	large pinches of saffron threads
1½ lb	tomatoes
1 lb	raw, unpeeled jumbo shrimp
½ lb	chorizo sausages
¾ lb	green beans
2 lb	mussels
8–10	chicken legs, total weight about 1½ lb
	salt and pepper
¼ cup	olive oil
3½ cups	short-grain rice, such as Arborio
1½ quarts	water, more if needed
1–2 tbsp	chopped parsley for decoration (optional)

ORDER OF WORK

1 PREPARE THE INGREDIENTS

2 COOK THE PAELLA

1 PREPARE THE INGREDIENTS

1 Peel the onions, leaving a little of the root attached, and cut them lengthwise in half. Slice each half horizontally, then vertically, toward the root, leaving the slices attached at the root end. Finally, cut across the onion to make small dice. Peel and finely chop the garlic; slice the bell peppers into thin strips (see box, right).

4 Leaving the shrimp in their shells, pull off and discard their legs. Twist the central flange of each shrimp tail and pull gently to remove the dark intestinal vein. Rinse and dry them.

Shrimp are cooked in their shells for extra flavor

Saffron releases color and flavor into hot water

2 Put the boiling water in a small bowl and sprinkle in the saffron threads. Soak, at least 15 minutes.

3 Meanwhile, cut the cores from the tomatoes and score an "x" on the base of each. Immerse in boiling water until the skins start to split, 8–15 seconds, depending on their ripeness. Transfer at once to cold water. When cool, peel off the skins. Cut them crosswise in half, squeeze out the seeds, then coarsely chop each half.

Gently twist and pull central tail flange to remove intestinal vein from shrimp

HOW TO CORE AND SEED BELL PEPPERS, AND CUT THEM INTO STRIPS OR DICE

The cores and seeds of bell peppers should be discarded before cutting them into strips or dice.

1 With a small knife, cut around the core of the bell pepper. Twist the core, and pull it out.

2 Halve the pepper lengthwise, and scrape out the seeds. Cut away the white ribs on the inside.

3 Set each pepper half cut-side down, flatten it with the heel of your hand and, using a chef's knife, slice it lengthwise into thin strips. For dice, gather the strips together, and cut crosswise.

5 With the chef's knife, trim the chorizo sausages, and cut them crosswise, on the diagonal, into ³/₈-inch slices.

Smoked chorizo sausages have dark skins

6 With your fingers, snap off the stem ends from the beans, pulling away any strings from both sides. Gather several beans together in a pile and cut them crosswise, on the diagonal, into 1-inch pieces.

7 Scrub each of the mussels under cold running water, with the small stiff brush. Scrape the shells with the small knife, to remove any barnacles. Detach and discard any weeds or "beards" from the mussel shells.

! TAKE CARE !
Discard any mussels that have broken shells or that do not close when tapped.

2 COOK THE PAELLA

1 Season the chicken with salt and pepper. Heat the oil in the paella pan and sauté the chicken, turning once, until brown and partially cooked, 10–12 minutes. Transfer to a plate.

2 Add the sliced chorizo sausage to the oil in the pan and sauté until browned, 1–2 minutes on each side. Transfer to the plate using the slotted spoon, and reserve.

3 Add the diced onion and the red bell pepper strips to the pan; cook, stirring occasionally with the wooden spoon, until soft, 5–7 minutes. Stir in the rice and cook until the grains absorb the oil, 2–3 minutes.

Red bell pepper strips become slightly soft while sautéing

ANNE SAYS
"Frying the rice in oil helps to keep the grains separate during cooking."

4 Stir in the water, garlic, saffron with its soaking liquid, plenty of salt, and pepper. Push the chicken pieces down into the rice mixture. Scatter the chorizo sausage slices over the rice, followed by the chopped tomatoes, and then the green beans.

5 Arrange the shrimp and mussels on top of the beans. Bring to a boil. Simmer, uncovered, until all the liquid has evaporated and the rice is tender but slightly chewy, 25–30 minutes. Turn the pan 90° every 7 minutes so the paella cooks evenly.

! TAKE CARE !
Do not stir the paella during cooking or the rice will become sticky.

6 If the rice is undercooked when the liquid has evaporated, add a little more water, and continue simmering, a few minutes longer. Remove from the heat, and discard any mussels that have not opened. Cover with the dish towel, and let stand, 5 minutes.

🍽 **TO SERVE**
Sprinkle the paella with parsley, if you like, and serve on warmed plates.

Rice should be just tender, with separate grains

VARIATION

SEAFOOD PAELLA
In this version of paella, the chicken is replaced by squid.

1 Omit the green beans and chicken. Prepare the saffron, onions, garlic, tomatoes, and chorizo sausages as directed, substituting green bell peppers for the red, and using hard-shell clams in place of the mussels.
2 With the shrimp in their shells, hold each one, underside up, on a chopping board. Leaving the tail end intact, cut the shrimp in half to open in a butterfly shape. Remove the dark intestinal vein.
3 Rinse 3/4 lb cleaned squid and drain it. Cut the tentacles from the body and cut them into 2–3 pieces if large, or leave whole if small. Cut the body crosswise into 3/8-inch rings.
4 Cook the chorizo sausages, onions, green bell peppers, and rice as directed. Pour in the water, arrange the chorizo slices over the rice, followed by the shrimp, tomatoes, squid, 1 cup shelled fresh or defrosted green peas, and finally the clams. Cook and serve as directed.

ANNE SAYS
"Tradition has it that the diners wait for the paella, never does the paella wait for the diners!"

FIVE-SPICE FILLET OF SALMON

🍽 SERVES 4   🥣 WORK TIME 30–35 MINUTES   🍲 BAKING TIME 20–25 MINUTES

EQUIPMENT

chef's knife

slotted spoon

metal spatula

colander

small knife

wooden spoon

aluminum foil

vegetable peeler

large sauté pan with lid †

paper towels

large baking dish

small bowl

parchment paper

chopping board

INGREDIENTS

salmon fillets

dry white wine

ground fennel seed

leeks

Chinese five-spice powder

carrots

cayenne pepper

butter

zucchini

Salmon fillets are coated with spices, lightly pan-fried, then baked on a bed of julienne vegetables. I like to use Chinese five-spice powder, but the same method will also suit curry powder or your favorite blend of Indian spices.

GETTING AHEAD

The vegetables can be prepared up to 1 day ahead, and kept, covered, in the refrigerator. Do not assemble the casserole or cook the fish until just before serving.

SHOPPING LIST

³/₄ lb	carrots
1¹/₂ lb	zucchini
1¹/₂ lb	leeks
4 tbsp	butter, more if needed
	salt and pepper
4	skinless salmon fillets, weighing about 6 oz each
2 tbsp	dry white wine
	For the spice mixture
1 tbsp	Chinese five-spice powder
1 tbsp	ground fennel seed
1	pinch of cayenne pepper

† large frying pan with lid can also be used

ORDER OF WORK

1 PREPARE AND COOK THE VEGETABLE JULIENNE

2 PREPARE THE SALMON AND BAKE THE CASSEROLE

1 PREPARE AND COOK THE VEGETABLE JULIENNE

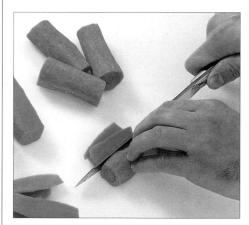

1 Peel and trim each of the carrots. With the chef's knife, cut them into 3-inch lengths, and square off the sides. Cut each piece lengthwise into fine slices.

Carrots are easy to slice thinly once sides are squared off

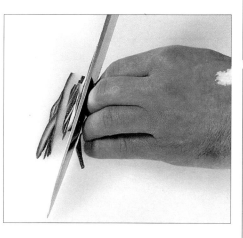

2 Stack the slices and cut them lengthwise into fine julienne, keeping the tip of the knife on the board as you slice.

3 Trim the zucchini and cut each of them into 3-inch lengths. Cut the peel from the zucchini, including about ¹/₈-inch of flesh.

4 Cut the slices of peel lengthwise into fine strips. Discard the interior pieces from the zucchini.

ANNE SAYS
"Cut vegetables into uniform, very fine strips so they will cook quickly and evenly."

5 Trim the leeks, discarding the roots and tough green tops. Cut them into 3-inch lengths, then cut lengthwise in half. Fan each half slightly, and cut lengthwise into thin julienne strips. Wash the strips in the colander very thoroughly.

Julienne should be cut into the finest possible slices

6 Melt half of the butter in the sauté pan. Add the leeks, carrots, salt, and pepper. Press a piece of buttered foil on top, cover with the lid, and cook gently, stirring occasionally, about 10 minutes.

7 Add the zucchini julienne, cover with the foil again, and continue cooking until all of the vegetables are tender, stirring occasionally, 8–10 minutes longer.

! TAKE CARE !
The vegetables should steam gently in their own juices without browning.

8 Remove the sauté pan from the heat. Transfer all the vegetables to the baking dish in an even layer, using the slotted spoon. Discard any liquid from the sauté pan. Allow the pan to cool slightly.

Lightly cooked vegetables retain vibrant color

Vegetables will form bed for salmon fillets

2 PREPARE THE SALMON AND BAKE THE CASSEROLE

1 Heat the oven to 400°F. Rinse the salmon fillets under cold running water and pat dry with paper towels.

2 Combine the Chinese five-spice powder, ground fennel seed, cayenne pepper, and a pinch of salt. Sprinkle the spices onto a sheet of parchment paper.

3 Coat the sides of each salmon fillet with the spice mixture, patting the fish gently with your hands so it is evenly coated.

4 Heat the remaining butter in the sauté pan. Cook the salmon over high heat, turning once with the metal spatula, 1–2 minutes on each side.

5 Transfer the salmon to the baking dish, using the metal spatula to place the pieces on the vegetables.

Sprinkling of white wine adds flavor

6 Sprinkle each salmon fillet with a little of the white wine. Bake the salmon and vegetables in the heated oven, 20–25 minutes.

7 When done, the salmon flesh should just flake when tested with a fork.

🍴 **TO SERVE**
Pile the vegetable julienne on warmed individual plates and set one salmon fillet on top of each. Decorate with lemon slices, if you like.

Vegetable julienne complements the flavor of spice-coated salmon

---

V A R I A T I O N

SALMON FILLETS WITH MUSHROOM AND LEEK JULIENNE

The spice coating is omitted to show off the pretty pink of the salmon, while a julienne of mushrooms replaces the carrots and zucchini.

1 Omit the zucchini, carrots, and spice mixture. Cut the leeks as directed. Wipe 3/4 lb mushrooms with damp paper towels and trim the stems even with the caps. Set the mushrooms stem-side down on a chopping board, and thinly slice them. Stack the slices and cut into very thin strips.

2 Cook the leeks as directed, add the mushrooms, and continue cooking, uncovered, until all the liquid from the vegetables has evaporated, 5–8 minutes longer.

3 Transfer the vegetables to individual baking dishes. Rinse the salmon as directed, season with salt and pepper, and set one fillet of fish in each dish of vegetables.

4 Sprinkle each piece of fish with a little of the white wine, and bake as directed.

Five-spice powder adds depth of flavor to salmon fillets

SEAFOOD AND TOMATO STEW

Cioppino

🍽 SERVES 4 🥄 WORK TIME 45–50 MINUTES ☕ COOKING TIME 20–25 MINUTES

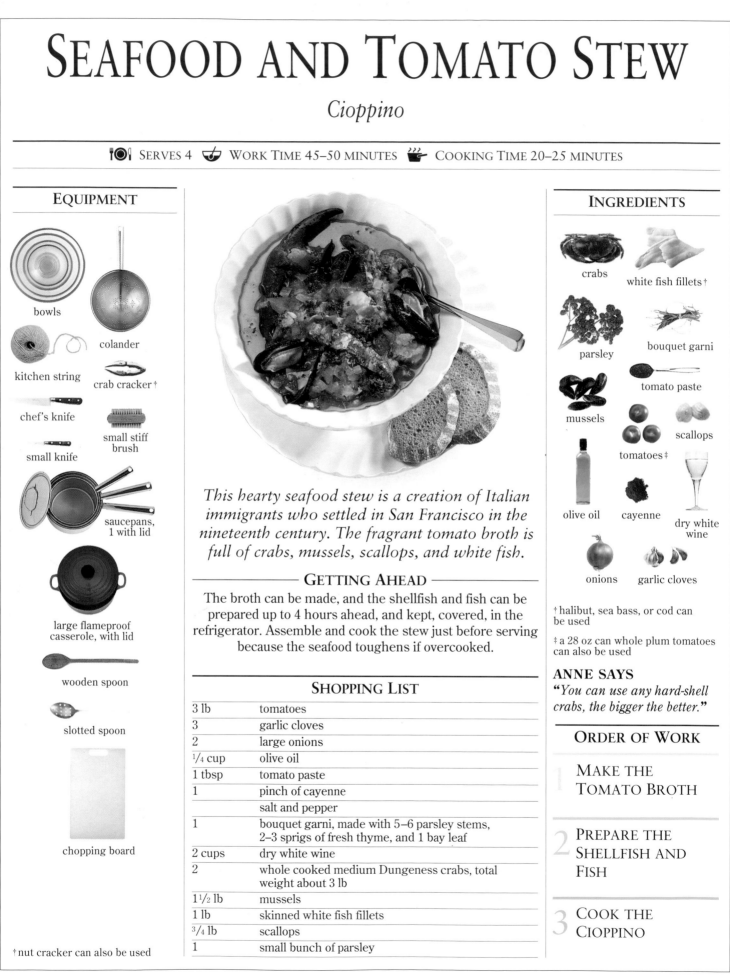

EQUIPMENT

bowls

colander

kitchen string

crab cracker †

chef's knife

small stiff brush

small knife

saucepans, 1 with lid

large flameproof casserole, with lid

wooden spoon

slotted spoon

chopping board

† nut cracker can also be used

INGREDIENTS

crabs

white fish fillets †

parsley

bouquet garni

tomato paste

mussels

scallops

tomatoes ‡

olive oil

cayenne

dry white wine

onions

garlic cloves

† halibut, sea bass, or cod can be used

‡ a 28 oz can whole plum tomatoes can also be used

ANNE SAYS
"You can use any hard-shell crabs, the bigger the better."

This hearty seafood stew is a creation of Italian immigrants who settled in San Francisco in the nineteenth century. The fragrant tomato broth is full of crabs, mussels, scallops, and white fish.

GETTING AHEAD

The broth can be made, and the shellfish and fish can be prepared up to 4 hours ahead, and kept, covered, in the refrigerator. Assemble and cook the stew just before serving because the seafood toughens if overcooked.

SHOPPING LIST

3 lb	tomatoes
3	garlic cloves
2	large onions
1/4 cup	olive oil
1 tbsp	tomato paste
1	pinch of cayenne
	salt and pepper
1	bouquet garni, made with 5–6 parsley stems, 2–3 sprigs of fresh thyme, and 1 bay leaf
2 cups	dry white wine
2	whole cooked medium Dungeness crabs, total weight about 3 lb
1 1/2 lb	mussels
1 lb	skinned white fish fillets
3/4 lb	scallops
1	small bunch of parsley

ORDER OF WORK

1 MAKE THE TOMATO BROTH

2 PREPARE THE SHELLFISH AND FISH

3 COOK THE CIOPPINO

30

MAKE THE TOMATO BROTH

1 Peel, seed, and chop the tomatoes (see box, right). Set the flat side of the chef's knife on top of each garlic clove, and strike it with your fist. Discard the skin and finely chop the garlic.

Garlic skin peels off easily if cloves have been lightly crushed beforehand

2 Peel the onions, leaving a little of the root attached, and cut them lengthwise in half. Lay each onion half flat on the chopping board and slice horizontally, then vertically, toward the root, leaving the slices attached at the root end. Cut across to make dice.

3 Heat the oil in a medium saucepan, add the onions, and cook until soft and translucent, 3–5 minutes.

4 Add the tomato paste, chopped tomatoes, garlic, cayenne, salt, pepper, and bouquet garni to the pan; pour in the white wine. Cover and simmer, stirring occasionally, about 20 minutes. Meanwhile, prepare the shellfish and fish.

White wine moistens tomatoes, onion, and garlic for broth

Bouquet garni of fresh herbs adds aromatic flavor

HOW TO PEEL, SEED, AND CHOP TOMATOES

Tomatoes are frequently peeled and seeded before chopping, so they need not be strained after cooking.

1 Bring a pan of water to a boil. Using a small knife, cut out the cores from the tomatoes. Score an "x" on the base of each. Immerse in the water until the skins start to split, 8–15 seconds depending on their ripeness. Using a slotted spoon, transfer them at once to cold water to stop cooking.

2 When cool, peel the skin from the tomatoes with a small knife. Cut them crosswise in half and squeeze out the seeds.

3 Set each tomato half cut-side down and slice it. Give it a half turn and slice again. Chop the flesh coarsely or finely, as required.

2 PREPARE THE SHELLFISH AND FISH

1 Set one of the crabs, back down, on the chopping board. Twist off each of the legs with your fingers, and reserve.

Large claws are full of succulent meat

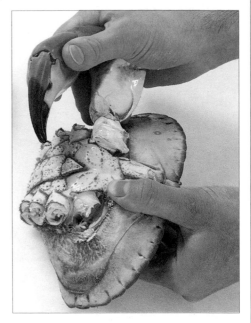

2 Holding the crab body steady, twist off the claws at the bottom joint, and reserve with the crab legs.

3 Using the crab cracker, crack the claws, leaving them whole and taking care not to crush the meat. If the legs are large, crack them also; discard them if they are small.

4 Open the body: with your fingers, lift off and discard the "apron" flap from the center of the shell.

5 With your thumbs, push along the "perforation," to crack the central section of the shell under the tail and prise it apart.

Body section separates easily from hard shell

Soft gills are known as "dead men's fingers"

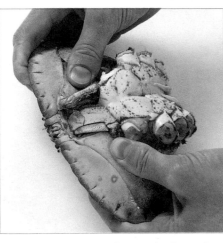

6 Gently pull the central body section away from the hard shell with one hand. Scrape out any soft brown meat from inside the shell, using a teaspoon, and reserve in a bowl; discard the shell.

7 With your fingers, pull off the soft gills from the central body section, and discard them.

8 Crack the central body section in half, using the chef's knife: while pushing the knife handle down with one hand, steady the end of the blade on the board with your other hand.

Apply pressure to knife with both hands to crack central body of crab

9 Pick out the meat from the central body section with the end of a teaspoon, discarding small pieces of cartilage. Add to the crab meat in the bowl and reserve. Repeat the whole process with the second crab.

Handle end of teaspoon is handy "pick" for removing crab meat

Crab meat flakes easily into bowl

10 Scrub the mussels thoroughly under cold running water with the small stiff brush.

11 Discard any mussels that have broken shells or that do not close when tapped.

Stringy "beards" must be removed from mussels

12 With the small knife, scrape the mussels to remove any barnacles. Detach and discard any weeds or "beards" from the shells.

13 Rinse the fish fillets under cold running water and dry them. Set the fish on the chopping board, and cut it into 2-inch pieces.

Fish is cut into large chunks so it holds its shape during cooking

Use sawing action to cut through fish without tearing flesh

14 If necessary, discard the tough, crescent-shaped membrane at the side of each scallop. Rinse the scallops in a bowl of cold water. Transfer to the colander, and let them drain thoroughly.

3 COOK THE CIOPPINO

1 Discard the bouquet garni from the broth. Taste and adjust the seasoning; it should be quite peppery.

2 Pack the fish pieces into the bottom of the casserole in an even layer, followed by the scallops. Arrange the crab meat and the cracked crab legs and claws over the scallops. Finally, cover with the mussels.

3 Ladle the hot tomato broth over the seafood and add water, if necessary, so the seafood is just covered. Cover the casserole with the lid, and bring to a boil. Simmer until the mussels have opened and the white fish flakes easily with a fork, 3–5 minutes.

Tomato broth permeates layers of seafood during cooking

ANNE SAYS
"*Do not overcook the stew or the shellfish will be tough and the white fish will fall apart.*"

Fish and shellfish should be covered

34

4 Meanwhile, strip the parsley leaves from the stems and pile the leaves on the chopping board. With the chef's knife, finely chop the leaves.

Peppery broth is rich with flavor of fish and shellfish

Opened mussel shells release their flavor into stew

5 Discard any mussels that have not opened. Taste the cioppino for seasoning and adjust if necessary.

🍴🍽🍷 TO SERVE
Transfer the cioppino to warmed bowls, with one crab claw in each bowl. Sprinkle with the chopped parsley. Serve immediately, with slices of sourdough bread, if you like.

Tomato broth joins with a variety of seafood in this full-flavored stew

Sourdough bread is traditional with cioppino for soaking up the tasty broth

FISH CIOPPINO

Traditional cioppino always includes shellfish, but I like to make this delicious stew using a variety of firm fish.

1 Make the tomato broth as directed. Omit the parsley. Chop the leaves from 1 small bunch of fresh basil.
2 Omit the crabs, mussels, and scallops. Prepare 1 lb halibut or cod fillets as directed. Discard the skin from 1 lb tuna steak, rinse with cold water, and pat dry with paper towels. Cut the tuna into 1-inch cubes.
3 Prepare 1 lb monkfish fillets: if necessary, remove the thin membrane that covers the flesh of the fillets. Rinse the monkfish under cold water and pat dry with paper towels. Holding the fillets steady, cut into diagonal slices, about 1/2-inch thick.
4 Layer the fish in a saucepan, starting with the monkfish, followed by the tuna, then the halibut or cod.
5 Add half of the basil to the tomato broth, then ladle the broth over the fish, and simmer until all the fish flakes easily with a fork, 10–12 minutes. Serve in warmed individual shallow bowls and sprinkle with the remaining basil. Breadsticks make a good accompaniment. Serves 6.

CHICKEN PAPRIKA WITH CARAWAY DUMPLINGS

ᵀᴼᴵ SERVES 4–6 ⌣ WORK TIME 40–45 MINUTES ♨ COOKING TIME 35–40 MINUTES

EQUIPMENT

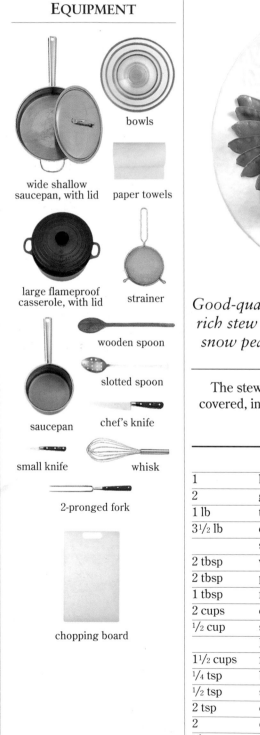

bowls

wide shallow saucepan, with lid

paper towels

large flameproof casserole, with lid

strainer

wooden spoon

slotted spoon

saucepan

chef's knife

small knife

whisk

2-pronged fork

chopping board

Good-quality Hungarian paprika is the key to this rich stew with caraway-seed dumplings. Steamed snow peas are a contemporary accompaniment.

GETTING AHEAD
The stew can be prepared up to 1 day ahead and kept, covered, in the refrigerator; add the sour cream and make the dumplings just before serving.

SHOPPING LIST

1	large onion
2	garlic cloves
1 lb	tomatoes
3½ lb	chicken, cut up into 8 pieces
	salt and pepper
2 tbsp	vegetable oil
2 tbsp	paprika, more to taste
1 tbsp	flour
2 cups	chicken stock (see box, page 57), more if needed
½ cup	sour cream
	For the caraway dumplings
1½ cups	flour
¼ tsp	baking powder
½ tsp	salt
2 tsp	caraway seeds
2	eggs
⅓ cup	water, more if needed

INGREDIENTS

chicken pieces

vegetable oil

flour

chicken stock †

paprika

caraway seeds

garlic cloves

onion

sour cream

baking powder

tomatoes

eggs

† water can also be used

ORDER OF WORK

1 **PREPARE THE DUMPLINGS AND VEGETABLES**

2 **COOK THE CHICKEN AND DUMPLINGS**

1 PREPARE THE DUMPLINGS AND VEGETABLES

1 Sift the flour, baking powder, and salt together into a large bowl.

2 Mix in the caraway seeds. Make a well in the center of the flour mixture, using your fingers.

Caraway seeds add characteristic Hungarian flavor to dumplings

Eggs in batter make dumplings light

Flour will blend easily with eggs if drawn in gradually

3 In a small bowl, whisk the eggs together. Add to the well with about three-quarters of the water. Gradually draw in the flour, and stir just until combined. Add more water if the dough is dry. Cover and refrigerate while preparing the vegetables.

ANNE SAYS
"Add enough liquid so that the dough is moist, but not too soft."

4 Peel the onion, and cut it lengthwise in half. Set each half cut-side down, and slice horizontally, then vertically, toward the root. Cut across to make fine dice.

Curled fingers guide knife blade

Coarsely chopped tomatoes will cook down in stew

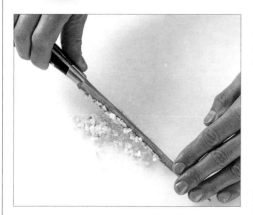

5 Set the flat side of the chef's knife on top of each garlic clove and strike it with your fist. Discard the skin and finely chop the garlic.

6 Cut out the cores and score an "x" on the tomatoes. Immerse in boiling water until the skins split, 8–15 seconds. Transfer to cold water. Peel and halve them; squeeze out the seeds, and coarsely chop.

2 COOK THE CHICKEN AND DUMPLINGS

1 Heat the oven to 350°F. Season the chicken pieces with salt and pepper. Heat the oil in the casserole on top of the stove. Working in batches, if necessary, add the chicken pieces to the casserole, skin-side down, and brown them well, about 5 minutes.

2 Using the 2-pronged fork, turn the chicken pieces, and cook the other sides until browned. Transfer the chicken to a plate and set aside.

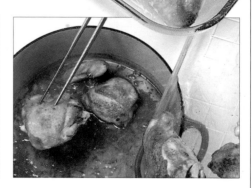

Browning chicken intensifies flavor of sauce

3 Add the chopped onion to the casserole, and cook over medium heat, stirring occasionally, until soft, 2–3 minutes. Add the garlic and continue cooking, 3–5 minutes longer.

4 Stir in the paprika. Cook very gently, stirring occasionally, about 5 minutes. Stir in the flour. Then add the tomatoes, chicken stock, salt, and pepper; bring the mixture to a boil.

5 Return the browned chicken pieces to the casserole. Cover with the lid, and cook in the heated oven until the chicken is tender when pierced with the 2-pronged fork, 35–40 minutes.

6 Meanwhile, cook the caraway dumplings: bring the shallow saucepan, filled with salted water, to a boil. Using 2 small spoons, dip them first in the boiling water, then use them to shape the dumpling dough into ³/₄-inch balls, and drop them into the boiling water.

ANNE SAYS
"If necessary, cook the dumplings in batches so the saucepan is not crowded."

Water should simmer but not boil vigorously

7 Cover the pan, and simmer until the dumplings are firm and cooked in the center, 7–10 minutes. Using the slotted spoon, transfer the dumplings to a plate lined with paper towels.

Dumplings become puffed and round as they cook

Center of dumplings should feel firm when fully cooked

8 Transfer the chicken pieces to a platter, and keep warm. Stir the sour cream into the sauce, and taste for seasoning. Add the dumplings to the casserole, and turn each one so it is coated in sauce. Cover the casserole, and cook very gently, about 2 minutes.

! TAKE CARE !
Do not heat the sour cream too vigorously, or it may curdle.

¶◉¶ TO SERVE
Divide the chicken among warmed plates; cover with the paprika sauce and dumplings.

Dumplings soak up the flavor and color of piquant paprika sauce

Crunchy green snow peas complement creamy stew

CHICKEN AND PAPRIKA PILAF

Long-grain rice and chicken marry in this rice pilaf perfumed with paprika and fresh oregano.

1 Omit the flour and sour cream, and substitute 4 boneless chicken breasts (total weight about 1¹/₂ lb) for the whole chicken. Omit the dumplings.
2 Strip the leaves from 7–10 sprigs of fresh oregano, reserving 4 top sprigs for decoration. Finely chop the leaves. Prepare the onion, garlic, and tomatoes as directed. Core, seed, and dice 1 green bell pepper.
3 Season the chicken with salt and pepper. Heat the oil in a casserole. Brown the chicken well on both sides. Transfer to a plate.
4 Lower the heat, add the onion, garlic, and pepper; cook as directed.
5 Stir in the paprika and cook, very gently, stirring occasionally, about 5 minutes. Add 1¹/₂ cups long-grain rice and cook, stirring, until the rice is slightly translucent, 2–3 minutes.
6 Add the chopped oregano, tomatoes, 2 tbsp tomato paste, 1 quart chicken stock or water, and the chicken breasts to the casserole. Cover, and cook in the heated oven until the chicken is tender and the rice is cooked, 20–25 minutes.
7 Taste for seasoning. Cut each chicken breast into 7–8 diagonal slices. Pile the rice on warmed plates, arrange the chicken on top, and decorate with the oregano sprigs. Serves 4.

CHICKEN AND BEER STEW

🍽 SERVES 4–6 🥣 WORK TIME 25–30 MINUTES 🍲 COOKING TIME 50–55 MINUTES

EQUIPMENT

large flameproof
casserole, with lid

rolling pin

plastic bag

wooden spoon

large metal spoon

chopping
board

2-pronged fork

chef's knife

small knife

paper towels

kitchen string

ANNE SAYS
*"You can use poultry shears
instead of a chef's knife for
cutting up the chicken, if you
prefer. They are especially
good for splitting the
breastbone, cutting the
backbone and rib bones, and
for cutting the breast and the
legs in half."*

*The inspiration for this stew comes from northern
Europe. The darker the beer, the richer this dish
will be. Mashed potatoes would be a good
accompaniment to the stew, and there's no
mystery what you should serve to drink with it!*

GETTING AHEAD

The stew can be prepared up to 2 days ahead and kept,
covered, in the refrigerator; the flavor will mellow. Reheat it
on top of the stove before serving.

SHOPPING LIST

1	chicken, weighing about 3½ lb
1½ lb	onions
1 lb	mushrooms
2 tsp	juniper berries
	salt and pepper
2 tbsp	butter
2 tbsp	vegetable oil
¼ cup	flour
3–4 tbsp	Cognac
1	bouquet garni, made with 5–6 parsley stems, 2–3 sprigs of fresh thyme, and 1 bay leaf
3 cups	dark beer
1	small bunch of parsley for garnish
¼ cup	heavy cream

INGREDIENTS

mushrooms

chicken†

flour

bouquet garni

parsley

butter

Cognac

vegetable
oil

dark beer

heavy
cream

onions

juniper
berries

†chicken already cut up into
8 pieces can also be used

ORDER OF WORK

**1 PREPARE THE STEW
INGREDIENTS**

2 COOK THE STEW

1 PREPARE THE STEW INGREDIENTS

Plastic bag stops juniper berries scattering on board

1 Cut up the chicken into 8 pieces (see box, below). Peel the onions, leaving a little of the root attached, then cut them lengthwise in half. Lay each half flat on the chopping board and cut across into thin slices.

2 Wipe the mushroom caps with damp paper towels and trim the stems even with the caps. Set the mushrooms stem-side down on the chopping board and, with the small knife, cut them into quarters.

3 Put the juniper berries inside the plastic bag. Holding the end of the bag closed in one hand, crush the berries gently with the rolling pin in order to release their flavor.

HOW TO CUT UP A CHICKEN INTO 8 PIECES

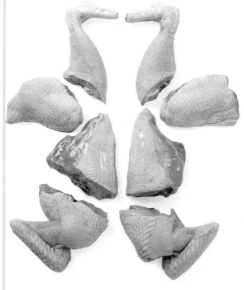

1 Using a chef's knife, cut down between one leg joint and the body. Twist the leg sharply outward to break the joint, then cut through it and pull the leg from the body. Repeat this procedure for the other leg.

2 Slit closely along both sides of the breastbone to loosen the meat, then split the breastbone. Turn the bird over onto its breast and cut along one side of the backbone. The bird is now divided in half.

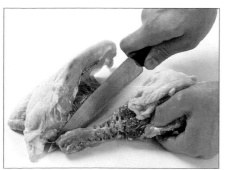

3 Cut the backbone and rib bones in one piece from the breast half where they are still attached, leaving the wing joints attached to the breast.

4 Cut each breast piece in half diagonally, cutting through the breast and rib bones so that a portion of the breast meat is included with the wing. Cut off any sharp bones.

5 Cut each leg in half through the joint, between the thigh and the drumstick, using the line of white fat around the joint as a guide.

2 COOK THE STEW

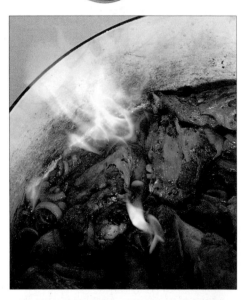

Remove chicken pieces as they brown

Heavy-based casserole gives even heat

1 Season the chicken pieces with salt and pepper. Heat the butter and oil in the casserole until foaming, and add the chicken pieces, skin-side down. Brown them well, about 5 minutes.

2 Turn the chicken pieces over using the 2-pronged fork, and brown the other side. Transfer the chicken to a plate and reserve.

3 Add the sliced onions and cook, stirring occasionally, until soft and well browned, 10–15 minutes. Sprinkle with the flour and cook, stirring, until the flour is just lightly browned, 1–2 minutes. Return the browned chicken to the pan in a single layer.

4 Add the Cognac. Set the alcohol alight with a lighted match. Baste the chicken with the Cognac until the flames subside, 20–30 seconds.

! TAKE CARE !
Flames can rise quite high, so stand back and use a long-handled spoon for basting.

5 Add the mushroom quarters, bouquet garni, and crushed juniper berries to the casserole. Pour in the beer.

Alcohol in beer evaporates during cooking, leaving rich concentrated taste

6 Bring to a boil, cover, and simmer until the chicken is tender when pierced with the 2-pronged fork and the juices run clear, 40–50 minutes.

7 Meanwhile, strip the parsley leaves from the stems and pile the leaves on the chopping board. With the chef's knife, finely chop them.

Cream, stirred into stew, gives sauce velvety consistency

8 Discard the bouquet garni from the stew and skim off excess fat from the surface using the large metal spoon.

9 Stir in the cream, and bring back just to a boil. Taste the stew for seasoning, and adjust if needed.

¶❍¶ TO SERVE
Transfer the stew to a warmed serving bowl, garnish it with the parsley, and serve immediately.

Mushrooms and onions add extra flavor to the chicken

Dark beer creates a rich flavorful sauce

VARIATION
CHICKEN WITH COGNAC

In this stew, chicken stock replaces beer, with baby onions instead of the sliced onions. Potatoes in chopped parsley are a good accompaniment.

1 Omit the mushrooms, onions, beer, juniper berries, cream, and parsley. Cut up the chicken as directed. Put 1 lb baby onions in a bowl, cover with boiling water, and leave, 2 minutes. Remove the onions and peel them, leaving a little of the root attached to hold the onion together while cooking.
2 Brown the chicken as directed and set aside. Add the baby onions to the casserole and cook, stirring, until golden brown, 5–7 minutes. Transfer the onions to a bowl.
3 Sprinkle the flour into the casserole and cook, 1–2 minutes. Replace the chicken and increase the heat to medium-high. Add 1 cup Cognac and bring to a boil. Hold a lighted match to the side of the casserole to set the alcohol alight. Baste the chicken with the sauce until the flames subside, 20–30 seconds.
4 Add 1 cup chicken stock, the baby onions, bouquet garni, salt, and pepper, and cook as directed.
5 Discard the bouquet garni and taste the stew for seasoning. Arrange the chicken on 4–6 warmed individual plates, spoon over the onions and sauce, and serve.

CHICKEN IN A POT

Poule au Pot

🍽 SERVES 4–6   🥣 WORK TIME 1 HOUR   🍲 COOKING TIME 1¼–1½ HOURS

EQUIPMENT

bowls

heatproof plate

aluminum foil

cheesecloth

kitchen string

paper towels

large metal spoon

vegetable peeler

slotted spoon

small knife

chef's knife

2-pronged fork

chopping board

whisk

strainers

saucepan

trussing needle

large flameproof casserole, with lid

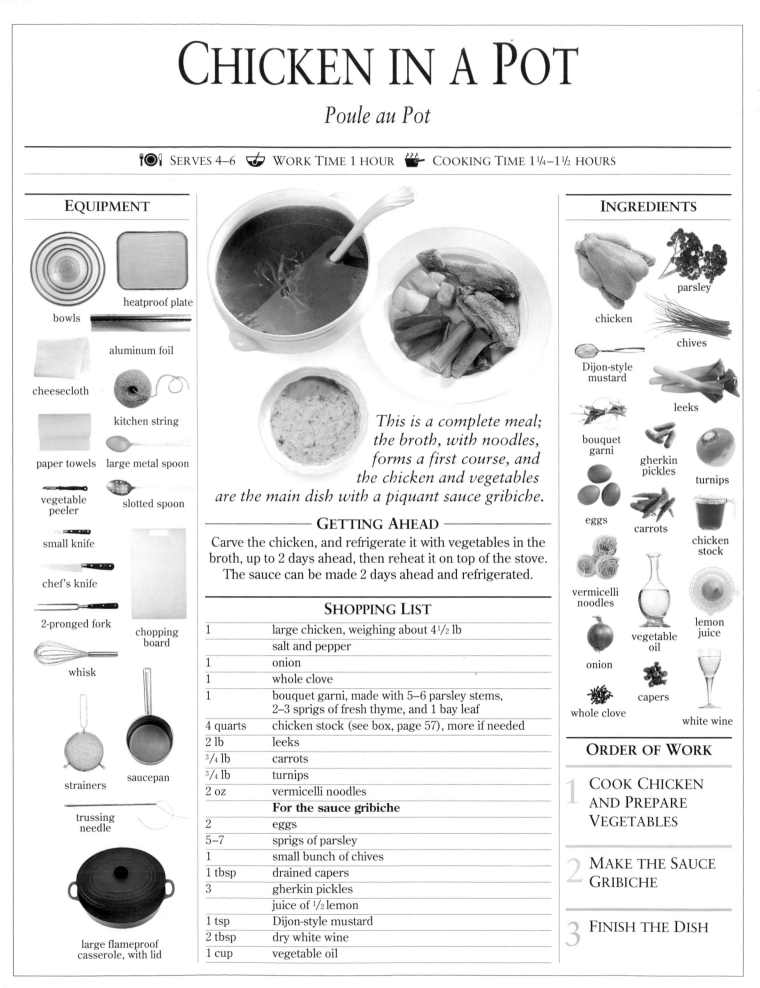

This is a complete meal; the broth, with noodles, forms a first course, and the chicken and vegetables are the main dish with a piquant sauce gribiche.

GETTING AHEAD

Carve the chicken, and refrigerate it with vegetables in the broth, up to 2 days ahead, then reheat it on top of the stove. The sauce can be made 2 days ahead and refrigerated.

INGREDIENTS

chicken

parsley

chives

Dijon-style mustard

leeks

bouquet garni

gherkin pickles

turnips

eggs

carrots

chicken stock

vermicelli noodles

vegetable oil

lemon juice

onion

capers

whole clove

white wine

SHOPPING LIST

1	large chicken, weighing about 4½ lb
	salt and pepper
1	onion
1	whole clove
1	bouquet garni, made with 5–6 parsley stems, 2–3 sprigs of fresh thyme, and 1 bay leaf
4 quarts	chicken stock (see box, page 57), more if needed
2 lb	leeks
¾ lb	carrots
¾ lb	turnips
2 oz	vermicelli noodles
	For the sauce gribiche
2	eggs
5–7	sprigs of parsley
1	small bunch of chives
1 tbsp	drained capers
3	gherkin pickles
	juice of ½ lemon
1 tsp	Dijon-style mustard
2 tbsp	dry white wine
1 cup	vegetable oil

ORDER OF WORK

1 COOK CHICKEN AND PREPARE VEGETABLES

2 MAKE THE SAUCE GRIBICHE

3 FINISH THE DISH

1 COOK CHICKEN AND PREPARE VEGETABLES

2 Put the chicken in the casserole. Add the bouquet garni and clove-studded onion; pour in enough chicken stock to cover the chicken by about three-quarters. Bring the stock to a boil, cover the casserole, and simmer, 45 minutes. Meanwhile, prepare the vegetables.

ANNE SAYS
"*The stock should just cover the thighs so that they cook more quickly and the tender breast does not overcook.*"

Stock surrounds chicken and ensures even cooking

1 Truss the chicken (see box, page 46). Trim the root and stem end from the onion, and peel it, using the small knife. Stud it with the clove.

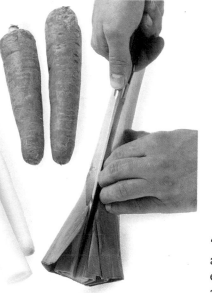

3 Trim the leeks, discarding the roots and tough green tops. Slit them lengthwise, with the chef's knife, and wash thoroughly under cold water. Cut them into 3-inch lengths, and put on a large piece of cheesecloth. Gather up the edges and tie securely with string to make a bundle that is easy to remove at the end of cooking.

Turnips should be firm and heavy in the hand

4 Trim the carrots and cut into 3-inch lengths. Halve them lengthwise and, using the small knife, trim the edges so they are rounded. Tie them in a piece of cheesecloth as for the leeks.

5 Peel the turnips and square off the sides; cut them into 1-inch slices. Stack the slices and cut into 1-inch strips. Gather the strips together and cut into 1-inch cubes. Tie them in cheesecloth as for the leeks.

Vegetable bundles will be easy to remove at end of cooking

6 Add the vegetable bundles to the chicken with more stock so they are covered. Cover the casserole, and simmer until the chicken and vegetables are cooked, 25–30 minutes longer. Meanwhile, make the sauce gribiche (see page 47).

HOW TO TRUSS A CHICKEN

1 Wipe the inside of the chicken with paper towels and season it, inside and out, with salt and pepper.

Hold chicken steady with one hand

2 Fold back the neck skin and, using the point of a small knife, remove the wishbone by cutting it out. Thread a trussing needle with string.

Chicken breast will be easy to carve into slices if wishbone is removed before cooking

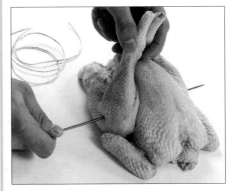

3 Set the bird, breast-side up; push the legs well back and down so the ends are straight up. Insert the trussing needle into the flesh at the knee joint, push it through the bird, and out through the other knee joint.

4 Turn the bird over. Pull the neck skin over the neck cavity, and tuck the wing tips over it. Push the needle through both sections of one wing, into the neck skin, and under the backbone to the other side. Repeat with the second wing.

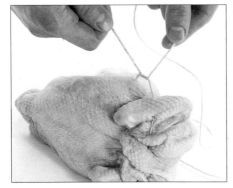

5 Turn the bird onto its side. Pull the string firmly together and tie securely. Turn the bird breast-side up. Tuck the tail into the cavity of the bird and fold over the top skin. Push the needle through the skin.

Chicken legs will not overcook once bird is trussed

6 Loop the string around one of the drumsticks, under the breastbone, and over the other drumstick. Tie the ends of string together securely.

ANNE SAYS
"Trussing keeps the chicken in shape so it cooks evenly."

Catch ends of drumsticks in loops of string

2 MAKE THE SAUCE GRIBICHE

1 Boil the eggs, 10 minutes. Drain, cool, and shell them. Rinse with cold water.

Egg shell comes off easily in your fingers

2 Dry the eggs and separate the yolks from the whites by gently pulling them apart. Cut the whites into strips, and finely chop them.

3 Put the yolks in a small strainer set over a bowl and work them through, using the back of a kitchen spoon. Scrape away the yolk clinging to the bottom of the strainer.

Finely chopped capers will blend into sauce

4 Strip the parsley leaves from the stems. Pile the leaves on the chopping board and finely chop them with the chef's knife. Gather the chives into a pile with your fingers, and finely chop them; mix them with the parsley.

5 With the chef's knife, finely chop the capers. Cut the gherkins crosswise into slices, then finely chop them, and mix with the capers.

6 Add the lemon juice to the egg yolks, with the mustard, salt, pepper, and white wine; whisk until combined. Gradually pour in the oil, while constantly whisking.

ANNE SAYS
"The sauce should emulsify and thicken slightly as you whisk."

7 Add the chopped egg whites, capers, gherkins, and herbs; whisk together to combine. Taste for seasoning.

3 FINISH THE DISH

1 Transfer the chicken to the chopping board, and remove the trussing string. Carve the chicken, using the chef's knife and the 2-pronged fork: cut down between one leg and the body. Turn the bird on its side, and cut around the "oyster" meat so it remains attached to the thigh. Twist the leg sharply outward to break the joint, then cut through it, and pull the leg from the body.

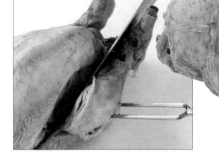

Hold chicken steady with 2 pronged fork while carving

Leg is easily cut away at bone joint

2 Halve the leg by cutting through the joint, using the line of fat on the underside as a guide. Repeat the procedure for the other leg.

3 Cut horizontally above one wing joint, through to the breastbone, so you will be able to carve whole slices from the breast. Cut off the wing. Repeat with the other wing.

4 Carve one breast in slices parallel to the rib cage. Carve the other breast in the same way. Put all the chicken pieces on the heatproof plate, cover with foil, and keep warm.

Carve breast diagonally into thin slices

Breast is easy to slice once leg and wing are removed

5 Remove the vegetables from the broth, with the slotted spoon, and keep warm, still in their cheesecloth.

6 Strain the broth into the saucepan, bring to a boil, and simmer until well flavored, 10–20 minutes. With the large metal spoon, skim off as much fat as possible, and taste the broth for seasoning. Add the vermicelli noodles to the boiling broth, and simmer just until tender, 3–5 minutes.

Broth is rich with flavor of chicken and vegetables

7 Meanwhile, cut the string from the bundles of carrots, leeks, and turnips, unwrap them, and discard the cheesecloth. Cover the vegetables, and keep them warm with the chicken until ready to serve.

Rich-flavored broth and noodles are served as a first course

🍴 **TO SERVE**

Serve the broth and noodles as a first course, reserving 1 cup broth. Serve the chicken and vegetables as a main course, with the reserved broth. Serve the sauce gribiche separately.

Chicken and vegetables form the main course of this complete meal

Sauce gribiche, with pickles and herbs, is a favorite accompaniment

---

V A R I A T I O N

TARRAGON CHICKEN

Here chicken is simmered with a generous amount of fresh tarragon, then the broth is transformed into a rich sauce.

1 Omit the leeks, carrots, and sauce gribiche. Truss the chicken as directed. Peel 1½ lb turnips, cut into cubes, and tie them in 2 cheesecloth bundles as directed.
2 Chop the leaves from 1 large bunch of fresh tarragon, reserving the stems.
3 Cook the chicken as directed, with the tarragon stems, stock, and the turnip bundles.
4 Carve the chicken as directed, cover, and keep warm. Lift out the turnips and keep warm.
5 Simmer the broth until reduced to about 2 cups. Melt ¼ cup butter in a saucepan. Whisk in ¼ cup flour and cook until foaming, 30–60 seconds. Remove from the heat and cool slightly, then strain in the broth, and whisk to mix.
6 Return to the heat and cook, whisking constantly, until the sauce thickens; simmer, 1 minute longer.
7 Add 1 cup heavy cream. Simmer until slightly thickened, 2–3 minutes. Stir in the chopped tarragon, and taste the sauce for seasoning.
8 Arrange the carved chicken and turnips on 4–6 warmed plates. Spoon some of the sauce over the chicken, and serve the remainder separately.

TURKEY MOLE

🍽 SERVES 8   🥣 WORK TIME 45–50 MINUTES   🍲 COOKING TIME 1¼–1¾ HOURS

EQUIPMENT

large flameproof casserole, with lid

small frying pan

saucepans

strainer

bowls

food processor †

chef's knife

small knife

2-pronged fork

vegetable peeler

rubber spatula

chopping board

wooden spoon

ladle

† blender can also be used

A blend of hot aromatic spices with bitter chocolate gives character to this Mexican turkey stew served with rice. Don't let the long ingredient list deter you; this famous dish is worth the attention.

SHOPPING LIST

1	celery stalk
2	onions
1	carrot
4	garlic cloves
¼ cup	vegetable oil
3½ lb	boneless turkey thighs
	salt and pepper
1 quart	water
1 tsp	black peppercorns
	For the mole purée
1 lb	tomatoes
1½ oz	unsweetened chocolate
1	slice of stale white bread
1	stale corn tortilla
1 cup	blanched almonds
½ cup	raisins
¼ cup	chili powder
1 tsp	each ground cloves, coriander, and cumin
¼ tsp	ground aniseed
2 tsp	ground cinnamon
¼ cup	sesame seeds

INGREDIENTS

carrot

tomatoes

raisins

vegetable oil

onions

blanched almonds

boneless turkey thighs

sesame seeds

chili powder

cinnamon

mixed spices

aniseed

celery

garlic cloves

black peppercorns

corn tortilla

white bread

unsweetened chocolate

ORDER OF WORK

1 COOK THE TURKEY AND FLAVORINGS

2 PREPARE THE MOLE PUREE

3 ASSEMBLE THE TURKEY MOLE

1 COOK THE TURKEY AND FLAVORINGS

1 Trim the celery stalk, peel off the strings with the vegetable peeler, and cut the stalk crosswise into quarters. Peel the onions and cut them into quarters. Peel the carrot and cut it crosswise into quarters.

Cut vegetables into large chunks so they will not break up during long cooking

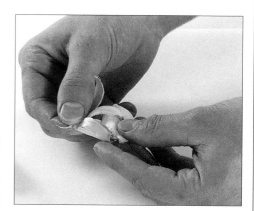

2 Set the flat side of the chef's knife on top of each garlic clove and strike it with your fist. Peel off and discard the skin.

Water should almost cover turkey and vegetables

3 Season the turkey pieces with salt and pepper. Heat half of the oil in the casserole. Add the turkey pieces, skin-side down. Brown them well, turning occasionally, 10–15 minutes.

Carrot adds slight sweetness to cooking liquid

4 Add the water, celery, 4 onion quarters, 1 garlic clove, the peppercorns, and carrot. Bring to a boil, cover, and simmer until the turkey is very tender when pierced with the 2-pronged fork, 45–60 minutes. Meanwhile, prepare the mole purée.

2 PREPARE THE MOLE PUREE

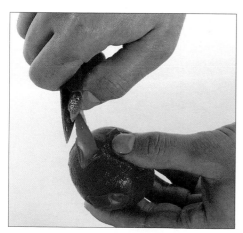

1 Core the tomatoes and score an "x" on the base of each with the tip of the small knife. Immerse in boiling water until the skins start to split, 8–15 seconds, depending on their ripeness. Transfer to cold water. When cool, peel off the skins. Cut them crosswise in half, squeeze out the seeds, then coarsely chop each half.

2 Break the chocolate into pieces and coarsely chop them. Tear the bread and tortilla into pieces.

3 Combine the tomatoes in the food processor with the remaining onion quarters and garlic, the bread, tortilla, almonds, raisins, chili powder, ground cloves, coriander, cumin, aniseed, cinnamon, and half of the sesame seeds. Work the ingredients to form a smooth purée.

ANNE SAYS

"*If the mixture is very thick, or you are using a blender, add ½ cup water and purée the mixture in 2 batches.*"

Almonds add body to mixture for mole purée

! TAKE CARE !
Different chili powders can vary greatly in strength, so be sure to check the type you are using before adding it to the mixture.

3 ASSEMBLE THE TURKEY MOLE

1 Remove the casserole from the heat, transfer the turkey thighs to a plate, and let cool slightly. Strain the cooking liquid into a bowl, discarding the vegetables.

2 When the turkey thighs are cool enough to handle, remove the skin and any fat, using the small knife. Pull the turkey meat into bite-sized pieces with your fingers.

Unsweetened chocolate adds depth of flavor to mole sauce

3 Heat the remaining oil in the casserole. Add the mole purée and cook, stirring constantly with the wooden spoon, until thick and dark, about 5 minutes.

4 Add the chocolate and cook, stirring constantly, to melt the chocolate into the purée, about 5 minutes longer.

5 Pour in the reserved cooking liquid, season with salt, and stir to combine. Simmer until the sauce begins to thicken, 25–30 minutes.

6 Meanwhile, toast the remaining sesame seeds: heat the frying pan, add the seeds, and toast them, stirring occasionally, until lightly browned, 2–3 minutes.

7 Return the turkey meat to the casserole and continue simmering until the sauce is thick enough to coat the back of the spoon, 10–15 minutes longer. Taste for seasoning.

Mole sauce should be dark and rich but not sticky

¶❂¶ TO SERVE
Serve in warmed individual bowls, around white rice. Sprinkle with the toasted sesame seeds; top the rice with shredded coriander and chopped chili pepper, if you like.

Warm flour tortillas are a good accompaniment to turkey mole

VARIATION
PORK MOLE

Mole sauce complements the mild flavor of pork, with a cooling accompaniment of sour cream.

1 Omit the turkey thighs, celery, carrots, and black peppercorns. Peel and quarter 1 onion. Peel 3 garlic cloves. Make the mole purée as directed. Cook the purée and chocolate, substituting 1 quart water for the turkey cooking liquid. Simmer until thickened, 25–30 minutes.

2 Meanwhile, trim the excess fat from 8 pork chops (weighing about 6 oz each), and season both sides with salt and pepper. Heat 2 tbsp oil in a large frying pan, add the chops, and cook over high heat until well browned, 1–2 minutes. Turn the chops, and brown the other side. Add the chops to the mole sauce, cover, and cook gently until the pork is tender when pierced with a 2-pronged fork, 1–1¼ hours.

3 Toast the sesame seeds as directed. Taste the mole for seasoning. Divide the pork chops and sauce among 8 warmed plates, sprinkle with the toasted sesame seeds, and top each serving with 1 tbsp sour cream. Serve with white rice tossed with shredded coriander and chopped chili pepper, and kidney beans; decorate with a coriander (cilantro) sprig, if you like.

GETTING AHEAD
The stew can be cooked 1–2 days ahead and kept, covered, in the refrigerator. Reheat it on top of the stove just before serving.

BABY CHICKENS WITH PLUMS AND CABBAGE

🍽 SERVES 6   🥣 WORK TIME 35–40 MINUTES   ♨ COOKING TIME 1¼–1½ HOURS

EQUIPMENT

large flameproof casserole, with lid

colander

large pot

bowls

kitchen string

chef's knife

2-pronged fork

small knife

aluminum foil

wooden spoon

slotted spoon

whisk

chopping board

Small whole birds are cooked en cocotte *with Savoy cabbage. Bacon adds a smoky flavor to the sauce, with an underlying sweetness coming from fresh purple plums.*

GETTING AHEAD

The casserole can be cooked up to 1 day ahead and kept, covered, in the refrigerator. Reheat the birds with the cabbage in a 350°F oven. Add the remaining plums and thicken the sauce just before serving.

SHOPPING LIST

6	baby chickens, each weighing about 1 lb
	salt and pepper
1	Savoy cabbage, weighing about 3 lb
1½ lb	purple plums
½ lb	lean thick-cut bacon
1	onion
1	whole clove
2 tbsp	vegetable oil
1	bouquet garni (see box, page 58)
1 cup	dry white wine
2 cups	chicken stock (see box, page 57) or water
2 tsp	arrowroot
1 tbsp	water

INGREDIENTS

baby chickens †   Savoy cabbage

bouquet garni   thick-cut bacon

arrowroot ‡   purple plums

whole clove   dry white wine

chicken stock   vegetable oil   onion

† Cornish hens can also be used
‡ potato starch can also be used

ANNE SAYS
"If 1 lb birds are not available, use 3 larger ones, and serve half per person."

ORDER OF WORK

1 TIE UP THE BIRDS

2 BLANCH THE CABBAGE

3 ASSEMBLE AND BAKE THE DISH

4 FINISH THE DISH

1 TIE UP THE BIRDS

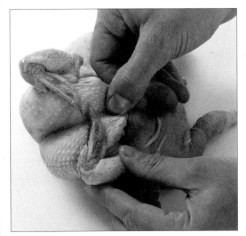

1 Season the insides of the chickens with salt and pepper. Hold one chicken, breast-side down, on a work surface, tuck the neck skin under the bird, and cover with the wings.

2 Turn the bird over and pass a length of string under the tail end of the bird; tie a secure knot over the leg joints.

ANNE SAYS
"Baby chickens hold their shape and cook evenly when they are tied up."

Use white kitchen string for tying

Cross ends of legs so they can be tied together easily

3 Bring the strings along the sides of the body, between the breast and the legs, and loop them around the legs.

Keep string pulled taut while tying up chicken

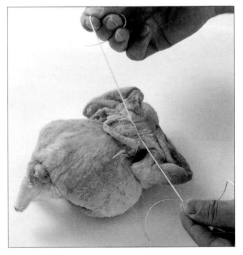

4 Turn the bird over so that it is breast-side down again, and tie the strings tightly under the body.

5 Bring both ends of the string down between the sides of the body and the insides of the wings.

6 Tie the wing bones at the neck opening so they are tucked securely under the body. Repeat the whole process with the remaining baby chickens and set aside.

2 BLANCH THE CABBAGE

1 With the chef's knife, trim off the stem end from the cabbage. Pull away the dark outer leaves, and discard them.

Discard dark leaves as they may be bitter

2 Cut the cabbage lengthwise in half. Set each half flat-side down on the chopping board, and cut it into quarters.

3 Rest the stem end of each quarter on the chopping board and cut out the core. Coarsely shred each quarter of cabbage and discard any tough ribs.

4 Fill the large pot with salted water, and bring to a boil. Add the cabbage, return the water to a boil, and simmer, 2 minutes. Drain the cabbage thoroughly in the colander.

3 ASSEMBLE AND BAKE THE DISH

1 With the small knife, cut the plums in half using the indentation on one side as a guide. Scoop out the pits with the knife and discard them.

2 Heat the oven to 350°F. Stack the bacon slices on the chopping board and cut crosswise into ½-inch strips, using the chef's knife.

3 Peel the onion, using the small knife, and stud it with the clove.

Turn birds so they brown evenly on all sides

4 Heat the oil in the casserole. Season the skin of the birds with salt and pepper. Brown them on all sides, turning them with the 2-pronged fork, 5–10 minutes. Transfer the birds to a plate. Reduce the heat, and let the casserole cool slightly.

5 Add the bacon to the casserole and cook, stirring occasionally, until the fat is rendered (melted), 3–5 minutes.

CHICKEN STOCK

Chicken stock is an indispensable ingredient in many sauces and stews. It keeps well, up to 3 days, covered, in the refrigerator, and it also freezes well. Stock is often reduced to concentrate the flavor for a recipe, so salt and pepper are not added while it is cooking.

🍴 MAKES ABOUT 2 QUARTS

🥣 WORK TIME 15 MINUTES

🍲 COOKING TIME UP TO 3 HOURS

SHOPPING LIST

1	stewing chicken
1	onion
1	carrot
1	celery stalk
1	bouquet garni, made with 5–6 parsley stems, 2–3 sprigs of fresh thyme, and 1 bay leaf
$1/2$–1 tsp	peppercorns
2 quarts	water, more if needed

1 Put the chicken in a large pan. Peel and quarter the onion and carrot; quarter the celery. Add to the pan with the bouquet garni and peppercorns.

2 Add water just to cover the ingredients. Bring to a boil and simmer, $1^1/4$–$1^1/2$ hours, skimming the stock occasionally.

3 Remove the stewing chicken from the pan of stock once the thighs are tender when pierced with a skewer. Continue simmering the stock, about $1^1/2$ hours longer.

Strain to remove flavoring ingredients

4 Using a ladle, strain the stock into a large bowl.

6 Spoon off all but 2 tbsp of fat. Stir in half of the cabbage with a little salt and pepper, and spread it evenly over the bottom of the casserole. Add the browned birds, and arrange two-thirds of the plum halves over them.

Blanched cabbage covers chickens and helps keep them moist

Chicken stock will form rich sauce with flavors from chicken, plums, and vegetables

Plums add fruity flavor to sauce

HOW TO MAKE A BOUQUET GARNI

This bundle of aromatic herbs is designed to be easily lifted and discarded at the end of cooking.

To make a bouquet garni, hold 2–3 sprigs of fresh thyme, 1 bay leaf, and 5–6 parsley stems together in your hand in a bundle. Wind a piece of string around the herbs a few times, and tie securely.

7 Add the clove-studded onion and bouquet garni. Cover with the remaining cabbage, and pour over the wine and stock. Cover, transfer to the oven, and bake until the birds are cooked and the juices run clear when the thighs are pierced with the 2-pronged fork, 45–55 minutes.

! TAKE CARE !
Be sure that the birds are thoroughly cooked.

8 Discard the onion and bouquet garni. Transfer the birds to the chopping board; remove the strings. Taste the cabbage mixture for seasoning.

Birds sit neatly on top of cabbage

Foil keeps birds warm and moist while finishing dish

9 With the slotted spoon, transfer the cabbage mixture to a warmed large serving dish. Set the birds on top, cover the dish with foil, and keep warm.

4 FINISH THE DISH

Plums should still hold their shape after simmering

1 Add the remaining plums to the cooking liquid and simmer until they are just tender, 5–8 minutes. Lift them out with the slotted spoon and arrange them with the chickens and cabbage in the center of the dish.

2 Boil the cooking liquid until well flavored and reduced by about half, 5–10 minutes. Stir the arrowroot and water together to form a smooth paste. Whisk enough of the paste into the liquid so it thickens to lightly coat the back of a spoon. Taste for seasoning.

¡©¡ TO SERVE
Spoon some of the sauce over the birds and pass the rest separately.

Baby chicken is ideal size for individual serving

BABY CHICKENS WITH CARROTS AND CABBAGE
Here, golden carrots replace the purple plums for satisfying country fare.

1 Omit the plums. Tie up the baby chickens, then shred the Savoy cabbage and blanch it, as directed.
2 Peel and trim 6 medium carrots (total weight about 1 lb); cut them into 2-inch lengths. Alternatively, trim the tops from 24 baby carrots, leaving about 1/2 inch of green. Scrape them with a small knife to remove the skin.
3 Brown the birds, and cook the bacon as directed. Mix half of the cabbage with the bacon in the casserole and season with salt and pepper. Top with the birds and all of the carrots, followed by the remaining cabbage.
4 Bake the casserole, and finish the sauce as directed. Serve the birds with the carrots on a bed of cabbage on warmed individual plates.

Plums add unusual fruity flavor to braised cabbage with bacon

Malaysian Chicken and Shrimp Stew

Laksa Lemak

🍽 SERVES 6 🥢 WORK TIME 35–40 MINUTES ☕ COOKING TIME 30–35 MINUTES

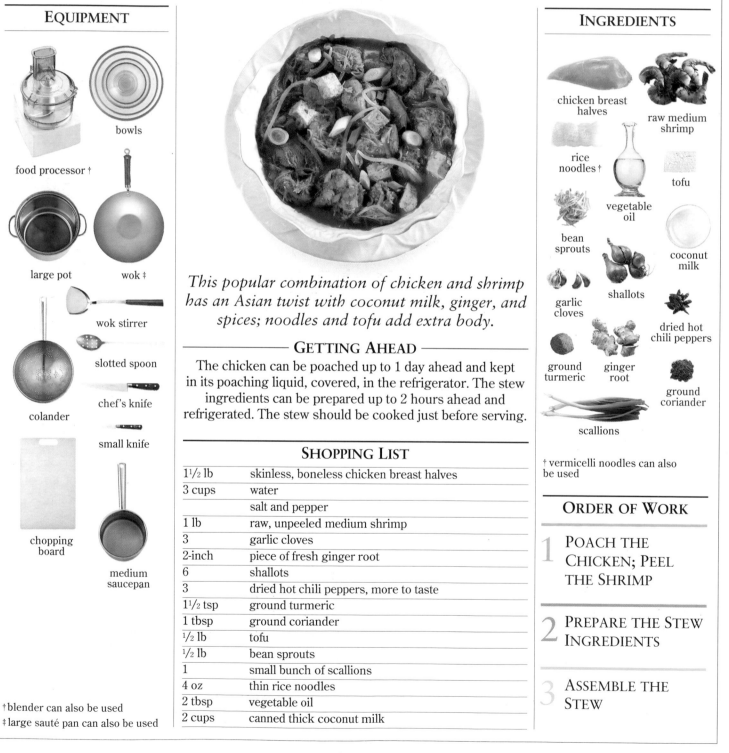

EQUIPMENT

bowls

food processor †

large pot

wok ‡

wok stirrer

slotted spoon

chef's knife

colander

small knife

chopping board

medium saucepan

† blender can also be used
‡ large sauté pan can also be used

This popular combination of chicken and shrimp has an Asian twist with coconut milk, ginger, and spices; noodles and tofu add extra body.

GETTING AHEAD

The chicken can be poached up to 1 day ahead and kept in its poaching liquid, covered, in the refrigerator. The stew ingredients can be prepared up to 2 hours ahead and refrigerated. The stew should be cooked just before serving.

SHOPPING LIST

1½ lb	skinless, boneless chicken breast halves
3 cups	water
	salt and pepper
1 lb	raw, unpeeled medium shrimp
3	garlic cloves
2-inch	piece of fresh ginger root
6	shallots
3	dried hot chili peppers, more to taste
1½ tsp	ground turmeric
1 tbsp	ground coriander
½ lb	tofu
½ lb	bean sprouts
1	small bunch of scallions
4 oz	thin rice noodles
2 tbsp	vegetable oil
2 cups	canned thick coconut milk

INGREDIENTS

chicken breast halves

raw medium shrimp

rice noodles †

vegetable oil

tofu

bean sprouts

coconut milk

garlic cloves

shallots

ground turmeric

ginger root

dried hot chili peppers

ground coriander

scallions

† vermicelli noodles can also be used

ORDER OF WORK

1 POACH THE CHICKEN; PEEL THE SHRIMP

2 PREPARE THE STEW INGREDIENTS

3 ASSEMBLE THE STEW

1 POACH THE CHICKEN; PEEL THE SHRIMP

1 Separate the small piece of fillet meat from each chicken breast, by pulling it off with your fingers. Strip the tendon from each fillet, stroking it with the small knife to remove it cleanly.

2 Bring the water to a boil in the saucepan; add the chicken breasts and fillets, salt, and pepper.

3 Simmer until the chicken is tender when pierced at the thickest portion and the juices run clear, 5–8 minutes for the fillets, 12–15 minutes for the breasts.

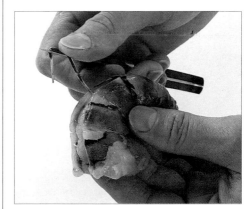

4 Meanwhile, peel off the shrimp shells with your fingers. Discard the shells. Make a shallow cut along the back of the peeled shrimp with the small knife, and remove the dark intestinal vein.

5 With the slotted spoon, transfer the chicken to the chopping board. Reserve the poaching liquid.

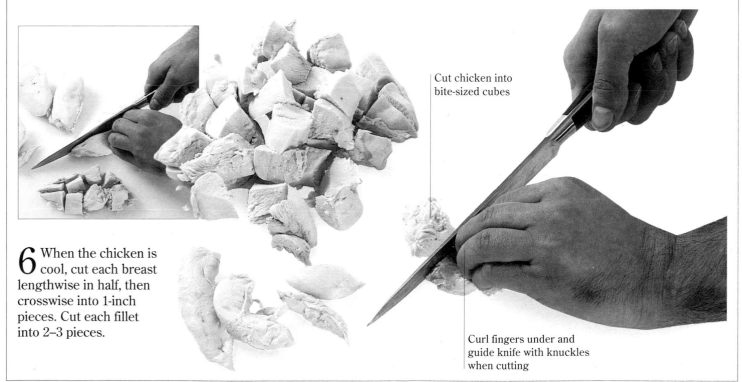

Cut chicken into bite-sized cubes

6 When the chicken is cool, cut each breast lengthwise in half, then crosswise into 1-inch pieces. Cut each fillet into 2–3 pieces.

Curl fingers under and guide knife with knuckles when cutting

HOW TO SOAK AND SEED DRIED HOT CHILI PEPPERS

When handling hot chili peppers, avoid contact with your eyes. For a hotter flavor, add the seeds.

1 Put the dried chili peppers in a bowl and pour over enough hot water to cover. Leave to soften, about 5 minutes, then drain.

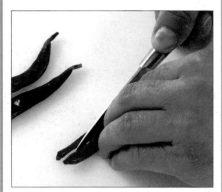

2 With a small knife, cut each of the soaked chili peppers lengthwise in half.

3 Holding the end of the chili pepper, scrape out the core, seeds, and white ribs from each half, using the small knife.

2 PREPARE THE STEW INGREDIENTS

1 Set the flat side of the chef's knife on each garlic clove and strike it with your fist. Discard the skin. Peel, slice, and crush the fresh ginger root (see box, page 64).

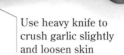

Use heavy knife to crush garlic slightly and loosen skin

2 Peel the shallots, separate them into sections, if necessary, and cut them into 2–3 pieces. Soak and seed the dried hot chili peppers (see box, left).

Ginger root is crushed before adding to food processor so it will be soft enough to purée

3 In the food processor, combine the garlic, shallots, chili peppers, turmeric, coriander, and crushed ginger slices; work the ingredients to a smooth paste.

ANNE SAYS
"If the mixture is very thick, add 2–3 tbsp of the chicken poaching liquid."

4 Drain the tofu in the colander, and discard the liquid. On the chopping board, cut the tofu into ½-inch slices using the chef's knife.

5 Stack the tofu slices and cut them lengthwise into ½-inch strips. Gather the strips together into a pile with your fingers, and cut crosswise into ½-inch cubes.

Fresh bean sprouts should be crisp

6 Pick over the bean sprouts and discard any that are brown. Trim the scallions and cut them into thick diagonal slices, including some of their green tops.

Cut scallions diagonally to make more attractive

Long thread-like rice noodles are very brittle before soaking

Rice noodles need only be soaked in boiling water

7 Fill the large pot with salted water, and bring to a boil. Add the rice noodles and remove the pan from the heat. Allow the noodles to soften until they are tender but still slightly chewy, 3–5 minutes, or according to package directions. Gently stir them occasionally to prevent them sticking to each other.

8 Drain the noodles in the colander, rinse under hot water, and drain again thoroughly.

HOW TO PEEL AND CRUSH FRESH GINGER ROOT

Fresh ginger root must be crushed to release its flavor throughout a dish. The crushed slices can then be chopped or puréed, if needed.

1 With a small knife, carefully peel the skin from the piece of fresh ginger root and discard it.

2 Using a chef's knife, slice the ginger, cutting across the fibrous grain.

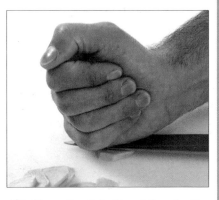

3 Place the flat side of the chef's knife on the slices of ginger and crush them by pressing firmly on the blade with your fist.

3 ASSEMBLE THE STEW

1 Heat the oil in the wok. Add the puréed ingredients, and cook gently, stirring constantly, until fragrant, 1–2 minutes.

ANNE SAYS
"The stirrer for the wok has a curved edge so it stays in constant contact with the wok surface."

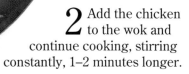
Sloping sides and round bottom of wok make it ideal shape for cooking evenly

2 Add the chicken to the wok and continue cooking, stirring constantly, 1–2 minutes longer.

3 Stir in the reserved poaching liquid and simmer until the mixture is rich and thickened, 20–25 minutes.

4 Add the shrimp and simmer, stirring occasionally, until they begin to lose their transparency and turn pink, 3–5 minutes.

5 Add the tofu, bean sprouts, and noodles. Pour in the coconut milk and stir to combine. Simmer very gently, about 5 minutes longer. Stir in half of the sliced scallions. Taste the stew for seasoning.

Thick coconut milk enriches stew

TO SERVE
Divide the stew between warmed individual bowls and sprinkle with the remaining sliced scallions.

Spicy sauce is aromatic, with a background of hot chili pepper

Rice noodles help to thicken the stew

THAI CHICKEN AND SHRIMP STEW

Thailand has an equally exotic stew, featuring lemon grass and fresh coriander (cilantro).

1 Omit the dried hot chili peppers, water, ground turmeric, ground coriander, bean sprouts, and tofu. Finely chop the leaves from 1 large bunch of fresh coriander (cilantro), reserving half of the stems.
2 Coarsely chop 2 stalks of lemon grass or grate the zest from 2 lemons. Peel 3 shallots. Prepare a 1-inch piece of fresh ginger root as directed.
3 In a food processor or blender, combine the garlic, lemon grass or lemon zest, ginger, shallots, and the reserved coriander stems. Work the ingredients to form a smooth paste.
4 Cut the chicken breasts crosswise into the thinnest possible slices.
5 Core, halve, and seed 2 fresh hot red chili peppers. Cut into very fine dice. Prepare the noodles as directed.
6 Squeeze the juice from 2 limes; you should have about 1/3 cup juice.
7 Heat the oil in a wok and cook the puréed ingredients as directed. Add the chicken, shrimp, salt, and pepper; stir-fry until the chicken and shrimp are cooked, 3–5 minutes.
8 Stir in 2 cups thick coconut milk, 2 cups chicken stock or water, the lime juice, and 1/4 cup Asian fish sauce (nam pla or patis). Simmer, 2 minutes, then add the chili peppers and coriander.
9 Stir in the noodles and simmer until just tender, 3–5 minutes. Taste for seasoning and serve in warmed bowls.

DUCK WITH TURNIPS AND APRICOTS

¶O¶ SERVES 4   WORK TIME 35–40 MINUTES   COOKING TIME 1½–2 HOURS

EQUIPMENT

bowls

large frying pan

poultry shears†

boning knife

chef's knife

2-pronged fork

small knife

wooden spoon

vegetable peeler

large flameproof casserole, with lid

chopping board

† chef's knife can also be used

This rustic preparation of duck combines turnips and apricots with Madeira wine to add the traditional touch of sweetness to the stew. Broad egg noodles are a perfect accompaniment.

GETTING AHEAD
The duck stew can be made up to 1 day ahead and kept, covered, in the refrigerator; the flavors will mellow. Gently reheat the stew on top of the stove.

SHOPPING LIST

1	duck, weighing about 4 lb
12–16	baby onions
1 lb	turnips
2	shallots
	salt and pepper
1 tbsp	vegetable oil
1 tbsp	butter
2 tbsp	flour
³/₄ cup	dry white wine
2 cups	brown veal stock (see box, page 109), more if needed
1	bouquet garni, made with 5–6 parsley stems, 2–3 sprigs of fresh thyme, and 1 bay leaf
1 tsp	sugar
1 cup	pitted dried apricots
¹/₄ cup	Madeira wine

INGREDIENTS

duck

pitted dried apricots

shallots

flour

baby onions

sugar

turnips

Madeira wine

dry white wine

bouquet garni

vegetable oil

veal stock †

butter

† water can also be used

ORDER OF WORK

1 CUT UP THE DUCK

2 PREPARE THE VEGETABLES

3 COOK THE STEW

1 CUT UP THE DUCK

1 Trim the excess fat and skin from the duck. Using the boning knife, cut down between one leg and the body of the duck. Twist the leg sharply outward to break the joint, cut through it, and cut the whole leg from the body. Repeat with the other leg.

Sharp knife cuts easily between duck leg and body

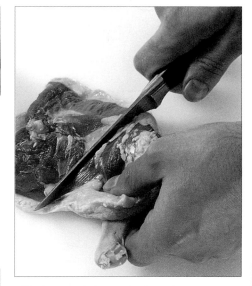

2 Cut each leg in half at the joint between the thigh and the drumstick, using the line of white fat on the underside as a guide.

3 Slit closely along both sides of the breastbone, to loosen the skin and meat from the bone. With the poultry shears or the chef's knife, cut along the breastbone to split it lengthwise in half.

4 Turn the bird over, and cut away the rib bones and backbone, in one piece, from the breast, leaving the breast pieces with the wing joints attached. Discard the back and rib bones.

5 Cut each breast piece diagonally in half, cutting through the breast and rib bones so that a portion of the breast meat is left with the wing joint. Cut off any sharp bones.

ANNE SAYS
"You can ask your butcher to cut up a duck for you, but the backbone may be included."

Cut breast into 2 equal pieces to cook evenly

2 PREPARE THE VEGETABLES

1 Put the baby onions in a bowl, cover with boiling water, and let stand, 2 minutes. Peel them, leaving a little of the root attached to hold them together.

2 Trim off the ends of the turnips and peel them using the vegetable peeler. Cut small turnips into quarters and large ones into eighths. With the small knife, trim off the sharp edges so they are rounded.

3 Peel the shallots, leaving a little of the root attached; separate them into sections, if necessary. Slice them horizontally, then vertically, toward the root, leaving the slices attached at the root. Cut across into fine dice.

3 COOK THE STEW

1 Heat the oven to 350° F. Season the duck pieces with salt and pepper. Heat the oil and butter in the casserole and add the duck pieces, skin-side down. Brown them well over low heat, 20–25 minutes. Turn the pieces and brown the other sides more quickly, about 5 minutes. Transfer to a plate and set aside.

ANNE SAYS
"The duck should be well browned so that the fat under the skin is thoroughly melted."

Pan should not be crowded when browning duck pieces

2 Transfer all but 2–3 tbsp fat from the casserole to the frying pan. Return the casserole to the heat. Add the flour, and cook, stirring constantly with the wooden spoon, until the mixture is lightly browned but not burnt, 1–2 minutes.

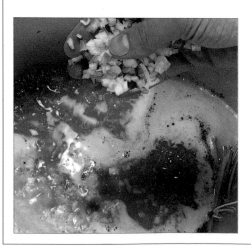

3 Add the white wine, stock, bouquet garni, salt, pepper, and chopped shallots to the casserole. Bring the mixture to a boil, and add the duck pieces. Cover, and cook in the heated oven, 40–45 minutes.

4 Meanwhile, heat the duck fat in the frying pan. Add the onions, turnips, sugar, salt, and pepper; cook, shaking the frying pan occasionally, until all the vegetables are evenly browned, 5–7 minutes.

5 Remove the stew from the oven; add the onions, turnips, and apricots. Stir in more stock if the sauce is very thick and the ingredients are not covered.

ANNE SAYS
"The dried apricots will plump and soften when cooked in the stew."

Add apricots and vegetables toward end of cooking so they will not overcook

Sauce is rich in flavor from veal stock

6 Cover, and continue cooking in the oven until the duck and vegetables are tender, 20–25 minutes longer. Skim off any fat from the surface. Stir in the Madeira wine, bring just to a boil on top of the stove, taste for seasoning, and adjust if needed.

Delicate chervil leaves add a splash of color to noodles

¶◎¶ TO SERVE
Serve the duck stew on warmed individual plates, on a bed of broad egg noodles, if you like.

Apricots, turnips, and baby onions garnish duck in Madeira sauce

VARIATION

DUCK WITH FRESH FIGS AND PORT WINE

Fresh figs replace the turnips and apricots in this duck stew, while port wine adds rich color and sweetness.

1 Omit the turnips, dried apricots, white wine, and Madeira wine. Cut up the duck, and prepare the shallots and baby onions as directed.
2 Cook the duck as directed, adding $3/4$ cup port wine with the veal stock, chopped shallots, bouquet garni, salt, and pepper.

3 Meanwhile, trim the stems from 1 lb fresh figs and cut the figs in half with a small knife.
4 Brown the onions as directed, add them to the stew, and cook, 5–10 minutes. Add the figs and cook the stew, 5–10 minutes longer. When the duck is tender, stir in $1/4$ cup more port wine, and bring back to a boil. Taste for seasoning and serve, decorated with thyme leaves, if you like.

INDIAN LAMB STEW

Dhansak

🍽 SERVES 6　🥄 WORK TIME 40–45 MINUTES　♨ COOKING TIME 1½–1¾ HOURS

EQUIPMENT

bowls

colander

chef's knife

wooden spoon

paper towels

slotted spoon

small knife

large flameproof
casserole, with lid

chopping board

*This spicy lamb stew is traditionally made with
no less than three different types of lentils and an
abundance of vegetables. My simple version is
based on lamb with* garam masala *(a spice
mixture), simmered with eggplant, cauliflower,
and a single kind of lentil. Fresh mango relish is
an optional, colorful accompaniment.*

GETTING AHEAD

The stew can be cooked 1–2 days ahead and kept, covered,
in the refrigerator. Reheat it on top of the stove. The mango
relish should be prepared no more than 2 hours ahead.

SHOPPING LIST

1	large eggplant, weighing about 1 lb
	salt and pepper
1	small cauliflower, weighing about 1½ lb
1½ lb	boneless lamb shoulder
5	garlic cloves
1	large onion
¾-inch	piece of fresh ginger root
¼ cup	vegetable oil
1 tbsp	flour
1½ quarts	water, more if needed
1 cup	green lentils
	mango relish (see box, page 72) for serving (optional)
	For the garam masala
2 tsp	each ground cumin, coriander, and turmeric
1	pinch of cayenne pepper

INGREDIENTS

boneless lamb
shoulder

cauliflower

green
lentils†

eggplant

garlic cloves

flour

onion

ground
coriander

ground
cumin

cayenne
pepper

ground
turmeric

vegetable oil

fresh ginger root

†brown or orange lentils can also
be used

ORDER OF WORK

1 PREPARE THE
INGREDIENTS

2 COOK THE
LAMB STEW

1 PREPARE THE INGREDIENTS

Cut eggplant into even-sized pieces

Leave skin on eggplant for more flavor

1 Trim and halve the eggplant lengthwise. Cut each half lengthwise into 4–5 strips. Cut the strips crosswise into 1-inch chunks. Put them in the colander and sprinkle generously with salt. Let stand to draw out bitter juices and soften, 30 minutes.

2 Meanwhile, cut the cauliflower florets from the stem and leaves, using the small knife. Put the florets in a bowl, cutting any of the large ones into halves or quarters.

3 Rinse the salt from the eggplant under cold running water, and drain well. Pat dry with paper towels.

4 Trim off any fat and sinew from the lamb, using the chef's knife, then cut the lamb into 1-inch cubes.

5 Set the flat side of the chef's knife on top of each garlic clove and strike it with your fist. Discard the skin and finely chop the garlic.

6 Peel the onion and cut it lengthwise in half. Set each half cut-side down and slice horizontally, then vertically, toward the root, leaving the slices attached at the root end. Cut across the onion to make dice.

7 Using the small knife, peel the skin from the fresh ginger root. With the chef's knife, slice the ginger, cutting across the fibrous grain. Crush each slice with the flat of the knife, then finely chop the slices.

Ginger is sliced across grain to cut through fibers

MANGO RELISH

This relish can be made 1–2 hours ahead, and the flavors will mellow.

🍽 MAKES ABOUT 1½ CUPS

🥣 WORK TIME 10 MINUTES

SHOPPING LIST

1	dried chili pepper
1	large mango, weighing about 1 lb
7–10	sprigs of fresh coriander (cilantro)
¼-inch	piece of fresh ginger root

1 Put the dried chili pepper in a small bowl, and cover with hot water. Let soften, 5 minutes, then drain. Cut the chili pepper lengthwise in half, discard the core, and scrape out the seeds.

2 Cut both chili pepper halves lengthwise into very thin strips, gather the strips together, and cut crosswise to produce very fine dice.

3 Cut the mango lengthwise into 2 pieces, slightly off-center so the knife just misses the pit. Repeat on the other side, leaving a little flesh around the pit. Discard the pit.

This neat method of cutting mango flesh is called "hedgehog"

4 With a small knife, slash the cut-side of one mango piece in a lattice, at ¼-inch intervals, cutting through the flesh but not the peel. Holding the mango flesh upward, carefully push the peel with your thumbs to turn it inside out, opening out the cuts.

5 Cut the cubes of mango away from the skin into a bowl. Repeat with the other mango piece. Strip the coriander leaves from the stems and finely chop the leaves. Peel, slice, and finely chop the ginger root.

6 In a small bowl, combine the mango cubes, chili pepper, ginger, salt, pepper, and chopped coriander leaves, and stir until mixed. Taste the mango relish for seasoning, cover, and chill, 30 minutes.

Golden mango relish is flecked with red chili pepper and green coriander

2 COOK THE LAMB STEW

1 Heat two-thirds of the oil in the casserole. Add some of the lamb pieces to the casserole, and season with salt and pepper. Cook over high heat, stirring occasionally, so the pieces brown evenly on all sides, 3–5 minutes.

2 With the slotted spoon, transfer the pieces of lamb to a bowl. Brown the remaining lamb in the same way.

3 Add the remaining oil to the casserole, then add the eggplant, and cook, stirring occasionally, until brown, 5–7 minutes. With the slotted spoon, transfer to a separate bowl.

4 Add the onions to the casserole and cook, stirring occasionally, until golden brown, 7–10 minutes. Stir in the garlic and ginger; cook until softened and fragrant, 2–3 minutes longer.

5 Stir in the ground cumin, coriander, turmeric, and cayenne pepper; cook, stirring constantly, until thoroughly combined, 1–2 minutes.

! TAKE CARE !
Be sure to cook the spices very gently so they do not scorch.

Flour coats lamb pieces and thickens stew slightly

6 Return the lamb with any juices to the casserole. Sprinkle with the flour and cook, stirring until blended, about 1 minute.

Turmeric in garam masala will color cauliflower vivid yellow

7 Stir in two-thirds of the water and bring to a boil. Lower the heat, cover, and simmer gently, stirring occasionally, 30 minutes. Stir in the lentils and cook, 15 minutes longer.

ANNE SAYS
"*Lentils will absorb a great deal of liquid as they cook, so you may need to add more water during cooking.*"

8 Stir in the eggplant, cauliflower, and the remaining water; continue simmering, stirring often, until the lamb is tender, and the lentils and vegetables are soft, 50–60 minutes. Add more water during cooking if the stew seems dry.

Saffron rice looks colorful in center of stew; extra rice can be served in separate bowls for each diner

¶◉¶ TO SERVE
Taste the stew for seasoning, transfer to a warmed platter, and garnish with shredded coriander leaves, if you like. Pass the mango relish separately.

Mango relish flavored with chili pepper adds heat and sweetness to stew

VARIATION

INDIAN CHICKEN STEW

The same spices flavor chicken, chickpeas, and vegetables in this stew. Serve it with Cucumber and Tomato Raita, a cooling relish that is traditionally served with hotter Indian dishes.

1 Omit the lamb, cauliflower, and lentils. Prepare the eggplant as directed. Peel, seed, and coarsely chop 1 lb medium tomatoes.

2 Sprinkle 1 chicken, cut up into 8 pieces (total weight about 3½ lb), with salt and pepper. Heat the oil in a large casserole, add the chicken, skin-side down, and cook until well browned, 5–7 minutes. Turn and brown the other side, then transfer to a plate.

3 Brown the eggplant as directed. Drain a 1 lb can of chickpeas.

4 Cook the stew as directed, adding the tomatoes and 1 quart water. Return the chicken to the casserole and simmer, 20 minutes.

5 Add the eggplant and chickpeas, then continue cooking, until the chicken is tender when pierced with a 2-pronged fork, 15–20 minutes longer. Taste the stew for seasoning, and transfer to a warmed serving dish. Serve with a bowl of raita (see box, below) and with some naan bread, if you like.

Chickpeas add substance and flavor to stew

Raita with yogurt is refreshing contrast to spicy stew

CUCUMBER AND TOMATO RAITA

🍽️ MAKES ABOUT 1½ CUPS

🥣 WORK TIME 15 MINUTES

SHOPPING LIST

1	small cucumber
1	small tomato
8	sprigs of fresh coriander (cilantro)
1 cup	plain yogurt
	salt and pepper

1 Coarsely grate cucumber, with its skin. Put it in a strainer set over a bowl. Squeeze it to remove as much juice as possible, and transfer to a bowl. Peel, seed, and chop the tomato. Finely chop the coriander leaves.

2 Mix the cucumber with the tomato, coriander, and plain yogurt. Season to taste with salt and pepper.

LAMB CHOPS CHAMPVALLON

🍽 SERVES 6   🥣 WORK TIME 25–30 MINUTES   🍲 BAKING TIME 2–2¼ HOURS

EQUIPMENT

2-pronged fork

chef's knife

vegetable peeler

large frying pan   pastry brush

wooden spoon

large metal spoon

pepper mill

9-x13-inch baking dish

large bowl

chopping board

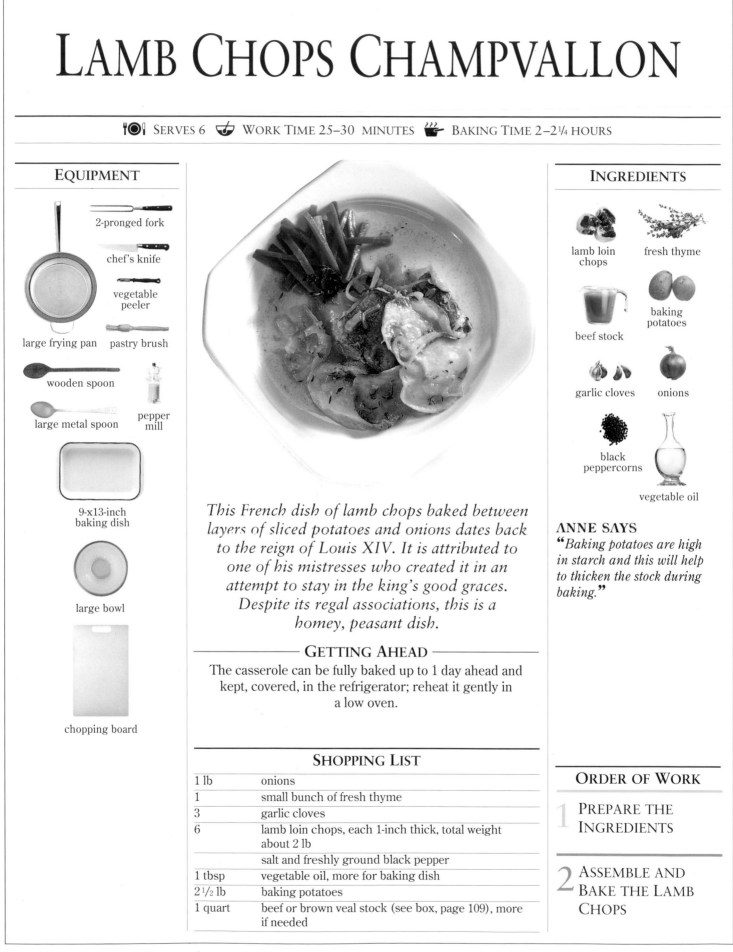

This French dish of lamb chops baked between layers of sliced potatoes and onions dates back to the reign of Louis XIV. It is attributed to one of his mistresses who created it in an attempt to stay in the king's good graces. Despite its regal associations, this is a homey, peasant dish.

GETTING AHEAD
The casserole can be fully baked up to 1 day ahead and kept, covered, in the refrigerator; reheat it gently in a low oven.

SHOPPING LIST

1 lb	onions
1	small bunch of fresh thyme
3	garlic cloves
6	lamb loin chops, each 1-inch thick, total weight about 2 lb
	salt and freshly ground black pepper
1 tbsp	vegetable oil, more for baking dish
2½ lb	baking potatoes
1 quart	beef or brown veal stock (see box, page 109), more if needed

INGREDIENTS

lamb loin chops

fresh thyme

beef stock

baking potatoes

garlic cloves

onions

black peppercorns

vegetable oil

ANNE SAYS
"Baking potatoes are high in starch and this will help to thicken the stock during baking."

ORDER OF WORK

1 PREPARE THE INGREDIENTS

2 ASSEMBLE AND BAKE THE LAMB CHOPS

1 PREPARE THE INGREDIENTS

1 Peel the onions, leaving a little of the root attached, then cut them lengthwise in half. Lay each onion half flat on the chopping board and cut across into thin slices.

2 Strip the thyme leaves from the stems, reserving a few sprigs for garnish. Peel and finely chop the garlic (see box, right).

Cut off most of fat, leaving thin layer around meat

3 Trim off the excess fat from the lamb chops, using the chef's knife. Season both sides with salt and pepper.

4 Heat the oil in the large frying pan, add the chops, and cook over high heat until well browned, 1–2 minutes on each side.

ANNE SAYS
"The chops should only be browned on the outside at this point; cooking will continue in the oven."

HOW TO PEEL AND CHOP GARLIC

The strength of garlic varies with its age and dryness; use more when it is very fresh.

1 To separate the cloves, crush the bulb with the heel of your hand or pull a clove from the bulb with your fingers. To peel the clove, lightly crush it with the flat side of a chef's knife to loosen the skin.

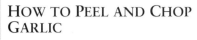

2 Peel off the skin from the garlic clove with your fingers.

3 To crush the clove, set the flat side of the knife on top and strike firmly with your fist. Finely chop the garlic with the knife, moving the blade back and forth.

Browning seals
in juices and
adds flavor to
lamb chops

5 Remove the chops from the frying pan, with the 2-pronged fork. Transfer to a plate and set aside.

6 Pour off all but about 1 tbsp of fat from the pan. Add the onions and cook over medium heat, stirring, until soft and translucent, 3–5 minutes. Remove the pan from the heat.

! TAKE CARE !
The onions should cook gently without browning too much.

Flavor from thyme
leaves infuses
vegetable mixture

Stir mixture gently
so potato slices do
not break

7 Peel the potatoes. Cut a thin slice from each potato so it sits flat on the chopping board. Cut the potatoes into very thin slices.

8 In the large bowl, gently stir the potato slices with the softened onions, thyme leaves, salt, and pepper.

2 ASSEMBLE AND BAKE THE LAMB CHOPS

1 Heat the oven to 350°F. Brush the baking dish with vegetable oil. Spread half of the potato mixture in an even layer in the dish. Sprinkle the chopped garlic over the potatoes.

Chopped garlic
perfumes potatoes
and lamb

2 Arrange the browned lamb chops in the baking dish on top of the sliced potato and onion mixture, spacing them out evenly.

3 Cover the lamb chops with the remaining potato mixture, arranging the potato slices neatly in rows. Pour over enough beef stock to come just to the top of the potatoes.

4 Transfer the dish to the heated oven and bake the casserole, uncovered, until the lamb chops and potatoes are tender when pierced with the 2-pronged fork, 2–2¼ hours.

ANNE SAYS

"The potatoes should be brown, and most of the liquid should have been absorbed. If the potatoes get dry before they are cooked, add more stock."

Beef stock almost covers potatoes to cook casserole evenly

🍽 TO SERVE

Divide the chops, potatoes, and onions among 6 warmed plates, and spoon over a little of the cooking liquid. Decorate with a sprig of thyme.

Glazed carrot sticks are a colorful accompaniment

Sliced potatoes should be crispy and brown

V A R I A T I O N

IRISH STEW

Leeks replace onions, creating this contemporary version of the famous Irish stew.

1 Omit the onions, garlic, and stock. Trim 1½ lb leeks, slit them lengthwise, and wash thoroughly. Cut into ½-inch slices, including some of the green.
2 Trim 6 lamb shoulder chops as directed. Slice 2 lb potatoes, then mix them with the thyme leaves, reserving a few leaves for garnish.
3 Brush a round casserole with oil. Spread half of the potatoes in the bottom of the casserole, followed by half of the sliced leeks; lightly season both layers with salt and pepper.
4 Season both sides of the lamb chops with salt and pepper, and set them on top of the leeks. Add the remaining leeks, then potatoes, seasoning each layer with salt and pepper.
5 Pour over water to just cover the potatoes, cover the casserole, and bake until the chops and potatoes are tender when pierced with the 2-pronged fork, 1¼–1½ hours.
6 Remove the lid from the casserole, and continue baking until the potatoes are lightly browned, about 30–45 minutes longer. Sprinkle the stew with the reserved thyme leaves and serve directly from the casserole.

BAKED HAM AND PRUNES IN RICH WINE SAUCE

🍽 SERVES 6 ⏲ WORK TIME 40–45 MINUTES 🍲 BAKING TIME 20–25 MINUTES

EQUIPMENT

large gratin dish

plastic bag

chef's knife

pastry brush

bowls

rolling pin

small knife

serrated knife

saucepans

wooden spoon

slotted spoon

ladle

whisk

chopping board

ANNE SAYS
"Use a heavy-based saucepan when making the syrup so the caramel does not burn."

I first tasted a version of this dish in the Chablis region of France, so white Chablis is the obvious wine to use, although any dry white will do. I've added prunes for natural sweetness and marc de Bourgogne, *a type of brandy that is distilled from grape crushings.*

GETTING AHEAD
The sauce can be made, and the dish assembled up to 1 day ahead. Keep it, covered, in the refrigerator and bake it just before serving.

SHOPPING LIST

1/2 cup	pitted prunes
1/4 cup	marc de Bourgogne
4	shallots
1/2 tsp	black peppercorns
3 tbsp	butter, more for gratin dish
2 tbsp	flour
1 cup	dry white wine
1 cup	beef stock (see box, page 109)
	salt
1/2 cup	heavy cream
2 lb	piece of cooked country ham
	For the vinegar and caramel syrup
1/2 cup	sugar
1/2 cup	water
1/2 cup	red wine vinegar

INGREDIENTS

shallots

cooked country ham

heavy cream

butter

pitted prunes

beef stock

sugar

black peppercorns

red wine vinegar

marc †

flour

dry white wine

†brandy can also be used

ORDER OF WORK

1 **MAKE THE VINEGAR AND CARAMEL SYRUP**

2 **PREPARE THE SAUCE**

3 **CARVE THE HAM AND FINISH THE DISH**

1 MAKE THE VINEGAR AND CARAMEL SYRUP

1 Gently heat the sugar and water in a heavy-based saucepan until the sugar dissolves. Increase the heat and boil, without stirring, until the syrup starts to turn golden around the edge.

2 Reduce the heat and cook until the syrup becomes a deep golden caramel. Remove the saucepan from the heat and let the bubbles subside.

3 Slowly add the vinegar. Simmer, stirring occasionally, to dissolve the caramel and reduce by half, 5–8 minutes. Remove from the heat.

! TAKE CARE !
The caramel splutters when the vinegar is added and the fumes will be strong; stand at arm's length when pouring.

2 PREPARE THE SAUCE

1 Halve the prunes, using the small knife, and put them in a small saucepan with the marc.

Pitted prunes are easy to cut in half

Dark-colored prunes will give sauce rich brown hue

2 Heat gently until the prunes are plump, 5–8 minutes. Using the slotted spoon, transfer the prunes to a plate; reserve the liquid.

3 Peel the outer, papery skin from the shallots, using the small knife. Finely chop them (see box, page 82).

4 Put the peppercorns in the plastic bag. Hold the end of the bag closed, and crush them gently with the rolling pin.

Plastic bag holds peppercorns conveniently for crushing

HOW TO CHOP A SHALLOT

For a standard chop, make slices that are about ⅛-inch thick. For a fine chop, slice the shallot as thinly as possible.

1 If necessary, separate the shallot into sections at the root and peel each section. Set each section, flat-side down, on a chopping board. Holding the shallot steady with your fingers, slice it horizontally toward the root, using a chef's knife, leaving the slices attached at the root end.

2 Slice vertically through the shallot, again leaving the root end uncut.

3 Cut across the shallot to make fine dice. Continue chopping, if necessary, until very fine.

5 Melt the butter in a medium saucepan. Add the chopped shallots and cook, stirring occasionally, until softened but not browned, 3–5 minutes. Stir in the flour and cook until foaming, 30–60 seconds. Remove the saucepan from the heat, and let cool slightly.

Shallots soften quickly in hot butter

6 Whisk in the white wine, return to the heat, and simmer, 1 minute. Add stock, prune soaking liquid, crushed peppercorns, and salt. Simmer, whisking constantly, until the sauce thickens and lightly coats the back of a spoon, 10–12 minutes.

7 Whisk the vinegar and caramel syrup into the sauce and continue simmering until it is again thick enough to coat the back of a spoon, 5–10 minutes longer.

Cream lightens color of sauce and mellows flavor

8 Stir in the heavy cream. Reserving a few prunes for garnish, add the remainder to the pan, and taste the sauce for seasoning.

ANNE SAYS
"Cooked ham is often salty, so additional salt may not be needed."

3 CARVE THE HAM AND FINISH THE DISH

1 Heat the oven to 350°F. Brush the gratin dish with melted butter. Holding the piece of ham steady with one hand, cut the ham across into 6 equal slices using the serrated knife.

Boneless cooked ham is easy to slice

ANNE SAYS
"Mark out even portions on the ham before you start slicing."

2 Arrange the ham slices evenly in the gratin dish, overlapping them slightly. Ladle over the sauce, so the ham slices are completely coated. Bake the ham in the heated oven until hot and bubbling, 20–25 minutes.

Sauce is piquant with peppercorns, white wine, and a sweet-sour syrup of vinegar and caramel

🍽 **TO SERVE**
Garnish the ham with the reserved prune halves and serve directly from the gratin dish with parsley potatoes, if you like.

Sweet prunes are delicious with salty baked ham

V A R I A T I O N

HAM WITH WHITE WINE AND APPLES

Apples flamed in Calvados add Norman flavor to this version of baked ham.

1 Omit the prunes and marc. Make the sauce as directed, omitting the vinegar and caramel mixture; set aside.

2 Core 4 apples with an apple corer. Cut 2 apples crosswise into 3/8-inch slices. Peel the remainder and cut them into dice.

3 Melt 1 tbsp butter in a frying pan. Add half of the apple slices, sprinkle with 1 tbsp sugar, turn, and sprinkle with an additional 1 tbsp sugar. Fry them until browned and caramelized, 2–3 minutes on each side. Remove and reserve for garnish. Repeat with the remaining apple slices.

4 Melt 2 tbsp more butter in the pan. Sauté the diced apples with 2 tbsp sugar, salt, and pepper until tender, 5–7 minutes.

5 Add 1/4 cup Calvados or brandy and bring to a boil. Flame the apples by holding a lighted match to set the alcohol alight. Shake the pan until the flames subside, 20–30 seconds.

6 Add the sauce to the apples and bring to a boil. Stir in the heavy cream, and taste for seasoning.

7 Bake the ham as directed. Serve topped with apple slices, and with fresh spinach, if you like.

BEEF, BARLEY, AND MUSHROOM STEW

🍽 SERVES 6–8 🥄 WORK TIME 30–35 MINUTES 🍲 COOKING TIME 2¼–2½ HOURS

EQUIPMENT

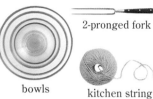

2-pronged fork

bowls

kitchen string

small knife

chef's knife

vegetable peeler

paper towels

large flameproof casserole, with lid

wooden spoon

slotted spoon

chopping board

Barley is a tasty grain that is all too often overlooked. Here it adds body and a characteristic earthy taste to a hearty beef and mushroom stew. For a treat, I like to replace some of the common mushrooms with fresh wild mushrooms.

GETTING AHEAD

The stew can be made 1–2 days ahead and kept, covered, in the refrigerator. Reheat it gently on top of the stove, adding more stock or water if it has thickened on standing.

SHOPPING LIST

3 lb	beef chuck steak
1¼ lb	onions
¾ lb	carrots
1 lb	mushrooms
4	celery stalks
3 tbsp	vegetable oil
	salt and pepper
1	bouquet garni, made with 5–6 parsley stems, 2–3 sprigs of fresh thyme, and 1 bay leaf
1 quart	beef stock (see box, page 109), more if needed
1 cup	pearl barley

INGREDIENTS

beef chuck steak

mushrooms

pearl barley

bouquet garni

celery stalks

carrots

onions

beef stock

vegetable oil

ANNE SAYS
"Pearl barley is the most common barley and needs no soaking before cooking."

ORDER OF WORK

1 PREPARE THE STEW INGREDIENTS

2 COOK THE STEW

1 PREPARE THE STEW INGREDIENTS

Cut beef into generous cubes so they remain moist during cooking

1 Using the chef's knife, trim off any fat and sinew from the beef and discard it. Cut the beef into thick slices, then cut crosswise into 2-inch cubes.

2 Peel the onions, leaving a little of the root attached, and cut them lengthwise in half. Lay each onion half flat on the chopping board, and cut crosswise into thin slices.

3 Peel and trim off the ends of the carrots; if large, cut the carrots lengthwise in half. Cut them crosswise into ¹/₂-inch slices. Clean and slice the mushrooms (see box, right).

Celery is very easy to slice once strings have been removed

4 Trim the celery stalks, peel off the strings with the vegetable peeler, and cut the stalks crosswise into ¹/₂-inch slices using the chef's knife.

HOW TO CLEAN AND SLICE MUSHROOMS

Mushrooms absorb moisture quickly, so do not soak them in water. In order to cook evenly, mushrooms should be cut into equal-sized pieces.

1 Wipe the mushroom caps with damp paper towels.

2 Trim the mushroom stems even with the caps.

3 Set the mushrooms, stem-side down, on a chopping board, and slice them vertically.

2 COOK THE STEW

Browned meat has sealed in juices

1 Heat the oven to 350° F. Heat the oil in the casserole on top of the stove. Add half of the beef and brown well on all sides. Transfer the meat to a bowl. Brown the remaining beef in the same way.

Cook meat in batches so it browns thoroughly on all sides

ANNE SAYS
"The oil should be hot enough so the meat sears when it is added to the pan."

2 Add the sliced onions with a little salt and pepper to the casserole. Cook over medium heat, stirring, until lightly browned, 5–7 minutes.

3 Add the beef, bouquet garni, salt, and pepper to the casserole. Pour in the beef stock and stir to combine.

4 Cover the casserole with the lid and transfer to the heated oven. Cook the stew, stirring occasionally, about 1½ hours.

5 Add the carrots, celery, and barley to the stew. Stir in more stock or water, if necessary, to keep the casserole moist.

Barley cooks at same rate as vegetables

ANNE SAYS
"Barley absorbs a great deal of liquid during cooking so more may need to be added."

6 Cover, and continue cooking until the meat and vegetables are tender when pierced with the 2-pronged fork, 40–45 minutes longer.

ANNE SAYS
"The barley should be tender but still be slightly chewy."

7 About 10 minutes before the end of cooking, add the sliced mushrooms and stir to combine.

Mushrooms are added toward end of cooking so they do not overcook

¶⊙¶ TO SERVE
Discard the bouquet garni, and taste the stew for seasoning. Serve in warmed individual bowls, with crusty bread, if you like.

Barley makes this stew a substantial winter meal

Stew should be well reduced, dark, and rich

BARLEY AND VEGETABLE STEW

A vegetable version of Beef, Barley, and Mushroom Stew. For a truly vegetarian dish, use vegetable broth instead of the beef stock.

1 Omit the beef. Prepare the onions, 1 lb carrots, 1 1/2 lb mushrooms, and 6 celery stalks as directed.
2 Cut the kernels from 4 ears of husked fresh corn: hold each ear vertically on a chopping board, and cut from the tip down to the board with a chef's knife. Turn the ear and continue removing as many whole kernels as possible. Alternatively, use 2 cups defrosted corn kernels.
3 Heat the oil in a large flameproof casserole, and sauté the onions with salt and pepper, stirring, until brown, 5–7 minutes. Stir in the stock, barley, carrots, celery, and bouquet garni.
4 Cover, and cook in the oven as directed, stirring occasionally, until the barley and vegetables are almost tender, 40–45 minutes. Add the mushrooms, corn, mushrooms, and 1 cup fresh or defrosted green peas; continue cooking until all the vegetables are tender, 10–15 minutes longer. Taste the stew for seasoning. Serve in warmed individual bowls.

PORTUGUESE PORK AND CLAM STEW

†❍❙ SERVES 6–8 **↩ WORK TIME 30–35 MINUTES*** **☕ COOKING TIME 2–2½ HOURS**

EQUIPMENT

large flameproof casserole, with lid

saucepan

chef's knife

small knife

bowls

2-pronged fork

paper towels

whisk

wooden spoon

slotted spoon

chopping board

small stiff brush

The combination of rich pork with salty clams has been enjoyed on the Iberian peninsula for centuries. In Portugal, a lemon wedge is squeezed over each serving just before eating.

GETTING AHEAD

The pork can be cooked without the clams 1–2 days ahead and kept, covered, in the refrigerator. Gently reheat the stew and cook the clams just before serving.

*plus 24 hours marinating time

SHOPPING LIST

3 lb	boneless pork loin
2 lb	hard-shell clams, such as littlenecks
1 lb	tomatoes
2	garlic cloves
1	large onion
1 tbsp	tomato paste
1	dash of Tabasco sauce, more to taste
1	lemon for serving
1	bunch of parsley for garnish
	For the marinade
2	garlic cloves
1	bay leaf
1½ tbsp	paprika
	salt and pepper
3 tbsp	olive oil
1½ cups	dry white wine, more if needed

INGREDIENTS

boneless pork loin †

bay leaf

clams

parsley

tomato paste

paprika

tomatoes

lemon

olive oil

dry white wine

Tabasco sauce

garlic cloves

onion

†pork shoulder can also be used

ORDER OF WORK

1 MARINATE THE PORK

2 PREPARE THE STEW INGREDIENTS

3 FINISH THE STEW

1 MARINATE THE PORK

1 Trim off excess fat and sinew from the pork, using the chef's knife. Cut the meat lengthwise into thick strips, and then cut crosswise into 1-inch cubes.

Some fat can be left on pork to flavor stew

2 Set the flat side of the chef's knife on top of each of the garlic cloves and strike it with your fist. Discard the skins, and finely chop the garlic; transfer to a large non-metallic bowl.

3 With your fingers, crumble the bay leaf into the bowl with the garlic. Discard the central stem of the leaf.

4 Add the paprika, plenty of black pepper, 1 tbsp oil, and the white wine; whisk to combine thoroughly. Add the pork and mix well. Cover and marinate in the refrigerator, stirring occasionally, 24 hours.

Wine in marinade will add depth of flavor to stew

2 PREPARE THE STEW INGREDIENTS

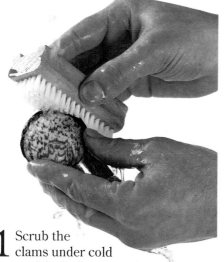

1 Scrub the clams under cold water with the brush, and discard any with broken shells, or that do not close when tapped.

2 Core the tomatoes and score an "x" on each. Immerse in boiling water until the skins split, 8–15 seconds. Transfer to cold water. Peel, halve, and seed them; coarsely chop each half.

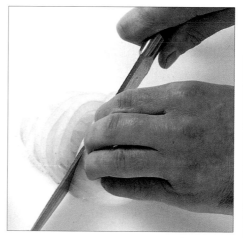

3 Peel and finely chop the garlic. Peel the onion, leaving a little of the root attached, then halve it lengthwise. Cut each half across into thin slices.

3 FINISH THE STEW

Paper towels absorb liquid so meat will brown evenly

1 Heat the oven to 350° F. Using the slotted spoon, transfer the meat from the marinade to a plate lined with paper towels; reserve the marinade. Pat the meat dry with paper towels.

2 Heat the remaining oil in the large casserole. Add the pork and brown well on all sides. With the slotted spoon, transfer the meat to a bowl.

ANNE SAYS
"Cook the meat in batches, if necessary, so that it browns thoroughly."

3 Lower the heat and add the onions and garlic, with a little salt, and pepper. Cover the casserole and cook very gently, stirring occasionally with the wooden spoon, until the onions are very soft and brown, 20–25 minutes.

Marinade doubles as cooking liquid for stew

4 Add the chopped tomatoes, tomato paste, Tabasco sauce, and the pork to the casserole. Pour in the reserved marinade and stir well.

5 Cover, and cook in the oven until the pork is tender when pierced with the 2-pronged fork, stirring occasionally, 1½–1¾ hours. Add more wine if the stew becomes dry.

6 Meanwhile, trim the ends from the lemon and cut it lengthwise in half. Lay each half cut-side down, and cut into 4 wedges.

7 Strip the parsley leaves from the stems and pile the leaves on the chopping board. With the chef's knife, coarsely chop the leaves.

Clams are cooked by steam from stew

8 Arrange the clams on top of the pork, cover with the lid, and continue cooking in the oven until the clams open, 15–20 minutes longer. Discard any clams that are still closed after cooking.

Salty clams are a delicious contrast to pork

TO SERVE
Transfer the stew to a warmed serving bowl. Sprinkle with chopped parsley. Serve the lemon wedges in a separate bowl.

Lemon is traditional accompaniment to pork and clam stew

CHILEAN PORK AND BEANS

To save time, you can use 4 cups canned red kidney beans instead of dried beans.

1 Omit the marinade and clams. Put 2 cups dried red kidney beans in a bowl. Cover with water, and let soak overnight. Drain and rinse.
2 Put the beans in a saucepan, cover with water and boil, 10 minutes. Reduce the heat, cover, and simmer until almost tender but still slightly firm, 3/4–1 1/2 hours. Drain well.
3 Meanwhile, prepare the tomatoes, garlic, and onion as directed. Core, seed, and dice 1 fresh hot green chili pepper and 2 green bell peppers.
4 Peel 1 lb each of sweet potatoes and yams and cut them into 1-inch cubes. Chop 7–10 sprigs each of parsley, coriander (cilantro), and oregano.
5 Brown the pork; cook the onions and garlic as directed. Return the pork to the pan. Add the tomatoes, tomato paste, herbs, and 2 cups water. Cover, and cook until the pork is just tender, 1 1/4–1 1/2 hours. Add the vegetables, beans, and 3 cups more water to cover.
6 Continue cooking, stirring occasionally, until tender, 40–45 minutes longer. Transfer the stew to the stove, stir in 2 tbsp red wine vinegar, and simmer, uncovered, 5 minutes. Taste for seasoning, and serve in warmed individual serving bowls.

FRENCH BEEF AND HERB POTATO PIE

Hâchis Parmentier aux Herbes

🍽 SERVES 6　　⤴ WORK TIME 45–50 MINUTES　　🍲 BAKING TIME 35–40 MINUTES

EQUIPMENT

food processor †

bowls

wooden spoon

pastry brush

slotted spoon

large sauté pan

colander

large shallow baking dish

vegetable peeler

saucepans, 1 with lid

metal skewer

rubber spatula

chef's knife

small knife

potato masher ‡

† blender can also be used

‡ potato ricer can also be used

A contemporary update of a French classic designed to use up the remains of a beef roast. This version uses fresh ground beef instead of leftover meat, with a topping of herb-flavored potato purée.

— GETTING AHEAD —

The pie can be assembled up to 1 day ahead and kept, covered, in the refrigerator. It should be baked just before serving.

SHOPPING LIST

1	large onion
³/₄ lb	tomatoes
4	garlic cloves
¹/₃ cup	olive oil
2 lb	ground beef
	salt and pepper
1 cup	beef stock (see box, page 109)
¹/₂ cup	dry white wine
	For the herb potatoes
2 lb	potatoes
1	bunch of fresh basil
1	bunch of parsley
1 cup	milk, more if needed

INGREDIENTS

parsley

basil

milk

ground beef

dry white wine

olive oil

tomatoes

onion

garlic cloves

beef stock †

potatoes

† water can also be used

ORDER OF WORK

1 COOK THE GROUND BEEF

2 MAKE THE HERB MASHED POTATOES

3 ASSEMBLE AND BAKE THE PIE

1 COOK THE GROUND BEEF

Skin peels easily from garlic if clove is partly crushed with knife

1 Peel the onion, leaving a little of the root attached; cut it lengthwise in half. Lay each half flat on a chopping board and slice horizontally, then vertically, toward the root, leaving the slices attached at the root end. Finally, cut across to make dice.

2 Core the tomatoes and score an "x" in each. Immerse in boiling water until the skins start to split, 8–15 seconds, depending on their ripeness. Transfer to cold water. When cool, peel and halve them crosswise. Squeeze out the seeds, and coarsely chop each half.

3 Set the flat side of the chef's knife on top of each garlic clove and strike it with your fist. Discard the skin and finely chop 2 of the cloves.

4 Heat one-third of the oil in the sauté pan, or in a frying pan. Add the onion and cook, stirring, until soft but not brown, 3–5 minutes.

5 Add the chopped garlic, ground beef, salt, pepper, and chopped tomatoes. Lower the heat, and cook very gently, stirring occasionally, until the meat is brown, 10–12 minutes.

6 Pour in the stock and white wine, and stir to combine. Continue simmering over very low heat, stirring occasionally, until most of the liquid has evaporated but the meat is still very moist, 25–30 minutes. Meanwhile, make the herb mashed potatoes (see page 94).

White wine adds rich flavor to meat mixture as alcohol cooks off

! TAKE CARE !
Do not cook the beef too fast or it will be tough and chewy.

2 MAKE THE HERB MASHED POTATOES

1 Peel the skin from the potatoes and cut each one into 2–3 pieces, depending on their size.

Vegetable peeler removes only very thin layer of flesh beneath skin

Hold potato firmly while peeling

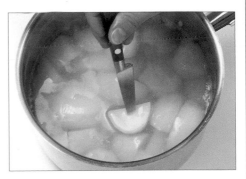

2 Put them in a saucepan with plenty of cold water, and add salt. Cover, and bring to a boil. Simmer until tender when pierced with the tip of the small knife, 15–20 minutes.

3 Meanwhile, strip the basil and parsley leaves from the stems. Put the leaves and the 2 whole garlic cloves in the food processor.

4 Work the herbs and garlic with the remaining oil to form a purée, scraping the side of the bowl occasionally.

ANNE SAYS
"If the purée sticks to the side of the processor, push it down with the rubber spatula, and add 3–4 spoonfuls of the milk."

5 Drain the potatoes and return them to the saucepan. Mash them with a potato masher. Alternatively, work them through a ricer. Add the herb purée to the potatoes.

6 Scald the milk in another saucepan. Gradually beat the milk into the potatoes over medium heat, and continue cooking and stirring until the potatoes just hold a shape, 2–3 minutes. Season to taste.

Stirring hot milk into potatoes lightens their texture

3 ASSEMBLE AND BAKE THE PIE

1 Heat the oven to 375°F. Brush the baking dish with oil. Taste the meat for seasoning, then spoon it, with any liquid, into the baking dish, in an even layer. Cover with the herb potatoes and smooth the top with the back of a spoon.

2 Make a scalloped pattern on the herb potatoes with the tip of a dessert spoon. Dip the spoon in a bowl of water occasionally so the potato does not stick to it.

Scalloped edges have golden crests

3 Transfer the pie to the heated oven and bake until the top is golden brown, and the skewer inserted in the center for 30 seconds is hot to the touch, 35–40 minutes.

🍽 TO SERVE
Cut the pie into 6 portions and transfer to warmed individual plates.

Meat filling is based on ground beef

Parsley and basil potatoes add a novel touch

VARIATION

OLD EMILY'S SHEPHERD'S PIE

I was brought up on shepherd's pie, made by our stout old housekeeper, Emily. She made it with leftover lamb or beef, but I like to use fresh lamb shoulder.

1 Omit the ground beef, wine, garlic, basil, parsley, olive oil, and tomatoes. Peel and trim 2 carrots, square off the sides, and cut them vertically into 1/4-inch slices. Stack the slices and cut into 1/4-inch strips. Gather the strips together and cut crosswise into cubes.
2 Heat 1 tbsp vegetable oil in a large sauté or frying pan; sauté the carrots and onions, until soft, 3–5 minutes; lower the heat, to cool the pan slightly.
3 Add 2 lb ground lamb, and brown very gently. Stir in 1 cup beef stock or water, with 1 sprig each fresh thyme and rosemary; simmer as directed.
4 Discard the herbs and taste the lamb mixture for seasoning.
5 Meanwhile, peel and cook 2 lb potatoes as directed. Drain them, and return them to the saucepan; mash them with a potato masher, and stir in 3 tbsp butter. Beat in the hot milk as directed. Season to taste with salt and pepper.
6 Brush 6 individual heatproof bowls with melted butter, and fill them with the lamb mixture. Divide the mashed potatoes among the bowls, and make a design on the top with a fork. Bake as directed until golden brown.

PEPPERY TUSCAN BEEF STEW

Stracotto di Manzo Peposo

🍽 SERVES 6   🥣 WORK TIME 35–40 MINUTES*   ♨ COOKING TIME 2–2½ HOURS

EQUIPMENT

- chef's knife
- small knife
- pastry brush
- slotted spoon
- large metal spoon
- bowls
- paper towels
- chopping board
- large pot
- wire rack
- baking sheet
- saucepan
- wooden spoon
- ladle
- serrated knife

INGREDIENTS

- beef chuck roast
- pancetta †
- garlic
- Italian bread
- plum tomatoes
- beef stock ‡
- onion
- black pepper
- bay leaves
- red wine
- fresh sage
- olive oil

† regular bacon can also be used
‡ water can also be used

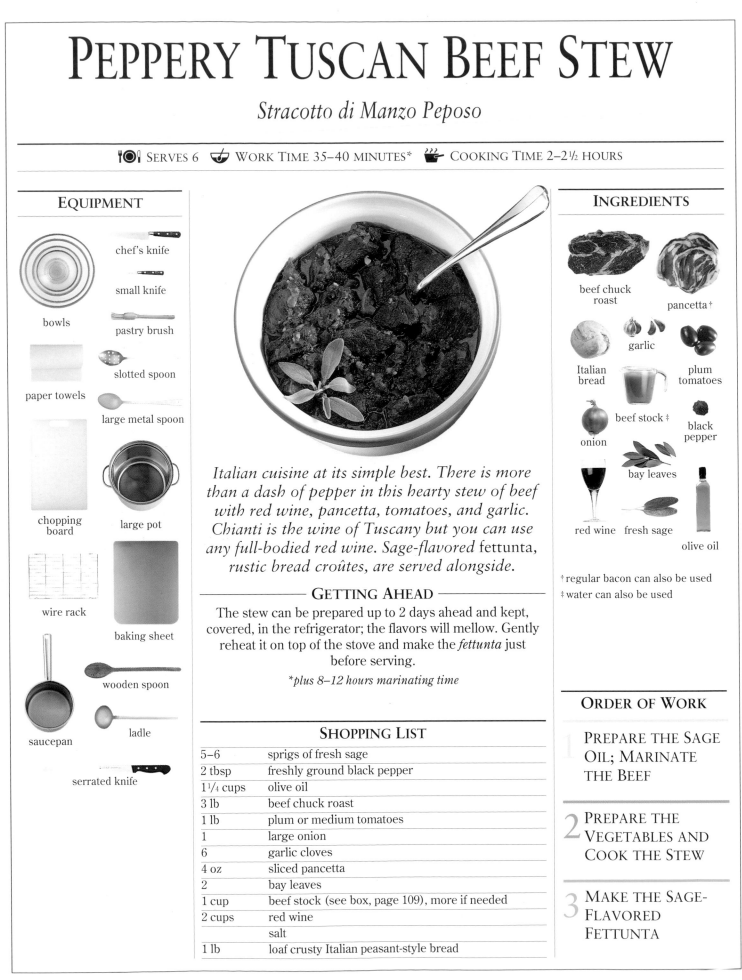

Italian cuisine at its simple best. There is more than a dash of pepper in this hearty stew of beef with red wine, pancetta, tomatoes, and garlic. Chianti is the wine of Tuscany but you can use any full-bodied red wine. Sage-flavored fettunta, *rustic bread croûtes, are served alongside.*

GETTING AHEAD

The stew can be prepared up to 2 days ahead and kept, covered, in the refrigerator; the flavors will mellow. Gently reheat it on top of the stove and make the *fettunta* just before serving.

*plus 8–12 hours marinating time

SHOPPING LIST

5–6	sprigs of fresh sage
2 tbsp	freshly ground black pepper
1¼ cups	olive oil
3 lb	beef chuck roast
1 lb	plum or medium tomatoes
1	large onion
6	garlic cloves
4 oz	sliced pancetta
2	bay leaves
1 cup	beef stock (see box, page 109), more if needed
2 cups	red wine
	salt
1 lb	loaf crusty Italian peasant-style bread

ORDER OF WORK

1 PREPARE THE SAGE OIL; MARINATE THE BEEF

2 PREPARE THE VEGETABLES AND COOK THE STEW

3 MAKE THE SAGE-FLAVORED FETTUNTA

PREPARE THE SAGE OIL; MARINATE THE BEEF

1 Chop the leaves from 2 of the sage sprigs (see box, below), and put them in a small bowl. In a large bowl, combine half of the black pepper with all but 3 tbsp of the oil. Ladle one-quarter of this mixture into the bowl with the chopped sage and set it aside for making the fettunta.

Some seasoned oil is reserved to brush on bread for fettunta

2 Trim and discard any fat and sinew from the beef. Using the chef's knife, cut the beef into 2-inch cubes.

Stir meat to moisten well with flavored oil

Chopped sage leaves will impart flavor to olive oil

3 Add the beef to the bowl with the black pepper and oil mixture. Stir until the beef is well coated with the oil. Cover, and leave to marinate in the refrigerator, stirring occasionally, 8–12 hours.

HOW TO CHOP HERBS

Sage, rosemary, parsley, dill, tarragon, and basil are herbs that are often chopped before being added to other ingredients. Do not chop delicate herbs like basil and tarragon too finely because they bruise easily.

1 Strip the leaves or sprigs from the stems. Pile the leaves or sprigs on a chopping board.

Leaves are pulled from woody stems

2 Cut the leaves or sprigs into pieces with a chef's knife, and chop the herbs, rocking the knife back and forth on the board.

2 PREPARE THE VEGETABLES AND COOK THE STEW

Use your knuckles to guide knife blade when chopping and slicing

1 Core the tomatoes and score an "x" on the base of each. Immerse in boiling water to split the skins, 8–15 seconds. Transfer to cold water. Peel and halve them, squeeze out the seeds, then coarsely chop each half.

2 Peel the onion, leaving a little of the root attached, and cut it lengthwise in half. Slice each half horizontally, then vertically, toward the root, leaving the slices attached. Cut across to make dice.

Chopped sage leaves will release their flavor into stew

Pancetta is traditional flavoring in Italian stews

3 Set the flat side of the chef's knife on top of each garlic clove and strike it with your fist. Discard the skin and finely chop 5 of the garlic cloves. Reserve the remaining garlic clove.

4 Chop the remaining sage leaves, reserving 2 sprigs for decoration. Stack half of the pancetta slices on the chopping board and thinly slice, then finely chop. Repeat with the remaining pancetta.

Marinated beef has absorbed oil and seasoning

Paper towels absorb excess marinade

5 Remove the meat from the marinade with the slotted spoon, and transfer to a plate lined with paper towels. Pat the meat dry with more paper towels.

6 Heat half of the remaining oil in the large pot over high heat, add half of the pieces of meat, and brown them well on all sides, 3–5 minutes.

Stir meat frequently to prevent sticking

Brown meat in batches so it colors well

! TAKE CARE !
The oil should be hot enough to sear the meat and brown it well.

7 Transfer the meat to a bowl with the slotted spoon. Add the remaining oil to the pot, and brown the rest of the beef in the same way.

ANNE SAYS
"Pancetta can be very salty, therefore the stew may not need any salt added."

8 Lower the heat to medium, add the chopped pancetta, and cook, stirring occasionally with the wooden spoon, until the fat is rendered (melted), 2–3 minutes.

Red wine adds richness and depth to stew

9 Add the chopped onion to the pot and cook, stirring, until softened, 3–5 minutes longer.

10 Return the beef to the pot with the garlic, tomatoes, bay leaves, sage, remaining black pepper, stock, and red wine.

11 Bring the stew to a boil, stirring to combine and dissolve the pan juices. Cover the pot, lower the heat, and simmer until the beef is very tender, stirring occasionally, 1¾–2 hours.

Stir while heating stew so pan juices are dissolved

12 During cooking, add more stock or water, if the stew seems dry. The beef is ready when it is tender enough to crush in your fingers.

Remove inedible bay leaves

13 Discard the bay leaves and taste the stew for seasoning. If the sauce is thin, increase the heat and boil, uncovered, until it is reduced and concentrated, 10–15 minutes.

3 MAKE THE SAGE-FLAVORED FETTUNTA

Brush bread generously with herb-flavored oil to crisp it in oven

1 Heat the oven to 375°F. With the serrated knife, cut the bread into ½-inch slices. Cut the large slices crosswise in half.

2 Set the bread on the baking sheet and brush generously with the sage-flavored oil, then sprinkle with salt.

Sage-flavored oil permeates toasted bread

3 Bake the bread in the heated oven until toasted, 7–10 minutes. Cut the reserved garlic clove in half.

4 Rub the toasted side of each bread slice all over with the cut side of the garlic clove and transfer to the wire rack. Discard the garlic.

Beef stew is rich with favorite Tuscan flavors

Crunchy fettunta are delicious with this hearty stew

🍴 TO SERVE
Spoon the stew into a warmed serving dish and decorate with the reserved sage sprigs. Serve with the sage-flavored fettunta, passed separately.

V A R I A T I O N

ITALIAN BEEF AND ROSEMARY STEW

In this beef stew, green olives and rosemary replace the piquant black pepper. Serve with rosemary fettunta.

1 Omit the pepper, pancetta, sage, and bay leaves. Coarsely chop the leaves from 1 large bunch of fresh rosemary. In a large bowl, combine half of the rosemary with all but 3 tbsp of the olive oil. Reserve 1/4 cup for the fettunta.

2 Cut the beef into cubes as directed, transfer to the large bowl and stir until well coated. Cover and marinate in the refrigerator, 8–12 hours.

3 Chop 5 garlic cloves as directed. Prepare the stew as directed, using 2 cups dry white wine instead of red, and adding the remaining rosemary in place of the bay leaves and sage.

4 Stir in the tomatoes and chopped garlic; cook until the meat is almost tender when pierced with a 2-pronged fork, 1 1/4–1 1/2 hours.

5 Add 1 cup oil-cured green olives; cook until the meat is very tender, about 30 minutes longer. If the sauce is too thin, uncover, increase the heat, and boil until concentrated, 10–15 minutes.

6 Meanwhile, make the fettunta as directed, with 1 garlic clove and the reserved 1/4 cup rosemary-flavored oil.

SPRINGTIME VEAL STEW

Blanquette de Veau Printanière

🍽 SERVES 6 🥣 WORK TIME 45–50 MINUTES ☕ COOKING TIME 1½–2¼ HOURS

EQUIPMENT

large flameproof casserole, with lid †

saucepan

colander

bowls

whisk

strainer

2-pronged fork

large metal spoon

slotted spoon

small knife

chef's knife

nutmeg grater

chopping board

† large saucepan can also be used

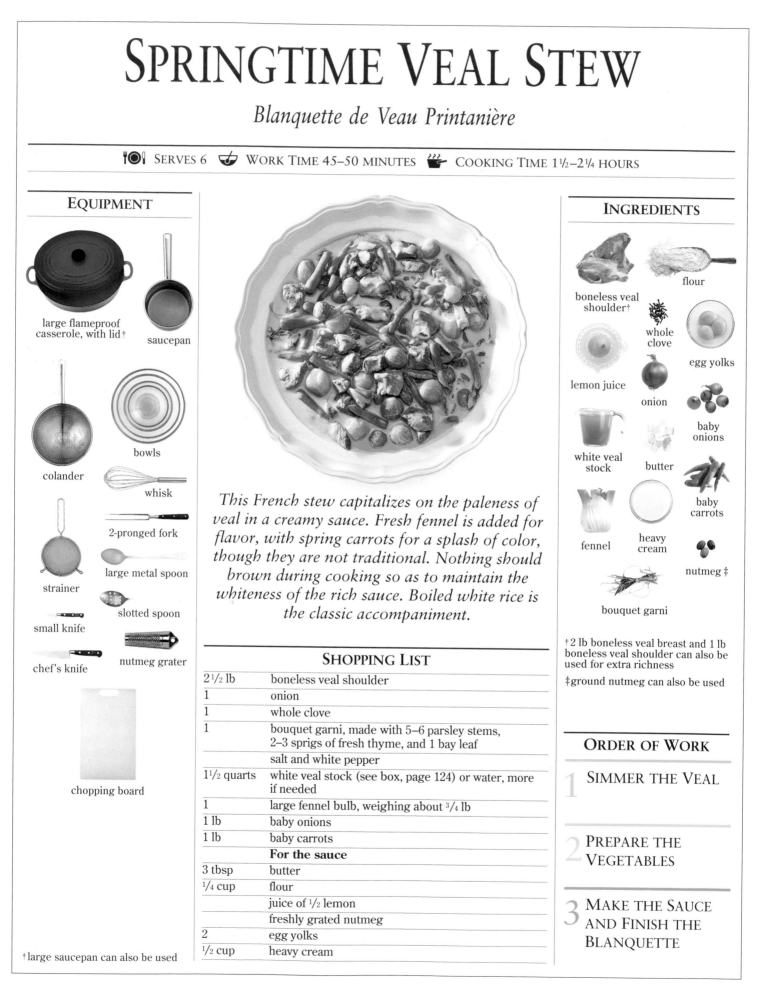

This French stew capitalizes on the paleness of veal in a creamy sauce. Fresh fennel is added for flavor, with spring carrots for a splash of color, though they are not traditional. Nothing should brown during cooking so as to maintain the whiteness of the rich sauce. Boiled white rice is the classic accompaniment.

INGREDIENTS

boneless veal shoulder†

flour

lemon juice

whole clove

egg yolks

onion

baby onions

white veal stock

butter

baby carrots

fennel

heavy cream

nutmeg ‡

bouquet garni

†2 lb boneless veal breast and 1 lb boneless veal shoulder can also be used for extra richness

‡ground nutmeg can also be used

SHOPPING LIST

2½ lb	boneless veal shoulder
1	onion
1	whole clove
1	bouquet garni, made with 5–6 parsley stems, 2–3 sprigs of fresh thyme, and 1 bay leaf
	salt and white pepper
1½ quarts	white veal stock (see box, page 124) or water, more if needed
1	large fennel bulb, weighing about ¾ lb
1 lb	baby onions
1 lb	baby carrots
	For the sauce
3 tbsp	butter
¼ cup	flour
	juice of ½ lemon
	freshly grated nutmeg
2	egg yolks
½ cup	heavy cream

ORDER OF WORK

1 SIMMER THE VEAL

2 PREPARE THE VEGETABLES

3 MAKE THE SAUCE AND FINISH THE BLANQUETTE

1 SIMMER THE VEAL

1 Using the chef's knife, trim and discard any fat and sinew from the veal. Cut the meat into 2-inch cubes.

2 Put the veal cubes into the saucepan, and cover with cold water. Bring to a boil, then reduce the heat and simmer, skimming often, 5 minutes. Drain the veal, rinse with cold water, and drain again.

3 Trim the onion and peel it with the help of the small knife. Stud the side of the onion with the clove.

4 Transfer the veal to the casserole. Add the bouquet garni, clove-studded onion, salt, and white pepper, and pour in the veal stock or water. Cover with the lid, bring to a boil, and simmer very gently, skimming occasionally, until the meat is almost tender, ¾–1 hour. Meanwhile, prepare the vegetables.

Veal stock adds flavor to blanquette but water gives whiter sauce

Herbs in bouquet garni infuse veal stew with fresh aroma

2 PREPARE THE VEGETABLES

Fennel adds pleasant anise flavor to stew

1 Trim the fennel, discarding any tough outer pieces. Cut the bulb lengthwise in half, set each half flat-side down on the chopping board and cut across into thin slices.

2 Trim and peel the baby onions (see box, page 104). Trim the baby carrots and scrape off the skin with the back of the small knife. Alternatively, peel and trim medium carrots, and quarter them lengthwise.

HOW TO PEEL BABY ONIONS

Leave a little of the stem and root on baby onions so that they hold together during cooking.

1 Put the baby onions in a medium bowl. Pour over enough hot water to cover, and let stand, 2 minutes.

2 Remove the onions from the water, one at a time, and peel them with a small knife, leaving a little of the stem and root attached.

---

3 Discard the clove-studded onion and the bouquet garni from the casserole. Add the fennel, baby onions, and carrots to the veal, with more stock or water, if needed, so that all the vegetables and the veal are covered.

ANNE SAYS
"Vegetables and veal should be well covered with stock to ensure even cooking."

Baby onions will remain intact during cooking

Baby carrots add touch of brilliant orange color to stew

4 Cover, and continue simmering until the veal and vegetables are tender when pierced with the 2-pronged fork, 20–30 minutes.

ANNE SAYS
"If the meat is cooked before the vegetables, remove the cubes and continue simmering the vegetables."

---

3 MAKE THE SAUCE AND FINISH THE BLANQUETTE

1 Remove the veal and vegetables. Strain the liquid into the saucepan, and simmer until well flavored and reduced by about half, 10–20 minutes.

2 Melt the butter in the casserole. Whisk in the flour, and cook until foaming, 30–60 seconds. Remove from the heat and cool slightly. Whisk in the cooking liquid, and return to the heat whisking constantly, until it boils and thickens, 3–5 minutes. Simmer until it coats the back of a spoon, 10–15 minutes.

! TAKE CARE !
If the sauce forms lumps at any stage, remove from the heat and whisk vigorously.

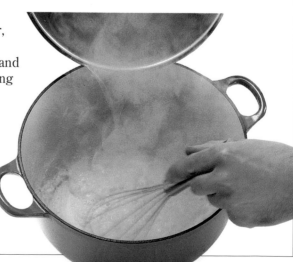

3 Return the veal and vegetables to the sauce and season to taste with the lemon juice, salt, white pepper, and grated nutmeg. Gently heat the blanquette so the flavors blend, 7–10 minutes longer.

ANNE SAYS
"Freshly grated nutmeg has a wonderfully aromatic flavor."

Very fine grater is used for grating fresh nutmeg

4 In a bowl, whisk together the egg yolks and cream until blended, then whisk in a few spoonfuls of the hot sauce. Stir this mixture back into the stew and heat gently, until the sauce thickens slightly, 1–2 minutes.

! TAKE CARE !
Do not boil the sauce or it will curdle.

TO SERVE
Transfer the stew to a warmed serving bowl, and serve immediately.

Velvety sauce is enriched with egg yolks and cream

Baby carrots and onions add sweetness to veal stew

FRENCH WHITE VEAL STEW

In this classic version of Blanquette de Veau, *the fennel and baby carrots are replaced by mushroom caps to make a whiter stew.*

1 Omit the fennel and carrots. Cook the veal as directed.
2 Prepare the onions as directed. Wipe $1/2$ lb button mushrooms with damp paper towels, and trim the stems even with the caps. Cut the mushrooms into quarters if large.
3 Put the mushrooms into a small saucepan with the lemon juice, $1/4$ cup water, salt, and pepper. Cover, and cook over high heat until the liquid boils to the top of the saucepan and the mushrooms are tender, 4–5 minutes. Drain the mushrooms and reserve the cooking liquid.
4 Cook the stew as directed, adding the mushrooms with the onions in place of the carrots and fennel. Stir the mushroom cooking liquid into the sauce when reducing it to a coating consistency. Finish as directed. Serve on warmed plates with boiled rice, and garnish with a fresh thyme sprig, if you like.

GETTING AHEAD
The stew can be prepared up to the addition of the egg yolks and cream, 1 day ahead, and kept, covered, in the refrigerator. Reheat the stew on top of the stove and finish the dish just before serving.

MOCK VENISON STEW

Jarret d'Agneau en Chevreuil

EQUIPMENT

- large flameproof casserole, with lid
- strainer
- non-metallic shallow dish
- large pot
- whisk
- rolling pin
- chef's knife
- small knife
- medium frying pan
- vegetable peeler
- wooden spoon
- slotted spoon
- large saucepan
- ladle
- 2-pronged fork
- bowls
- paper towels
- thick plastic bag
- conical strainer

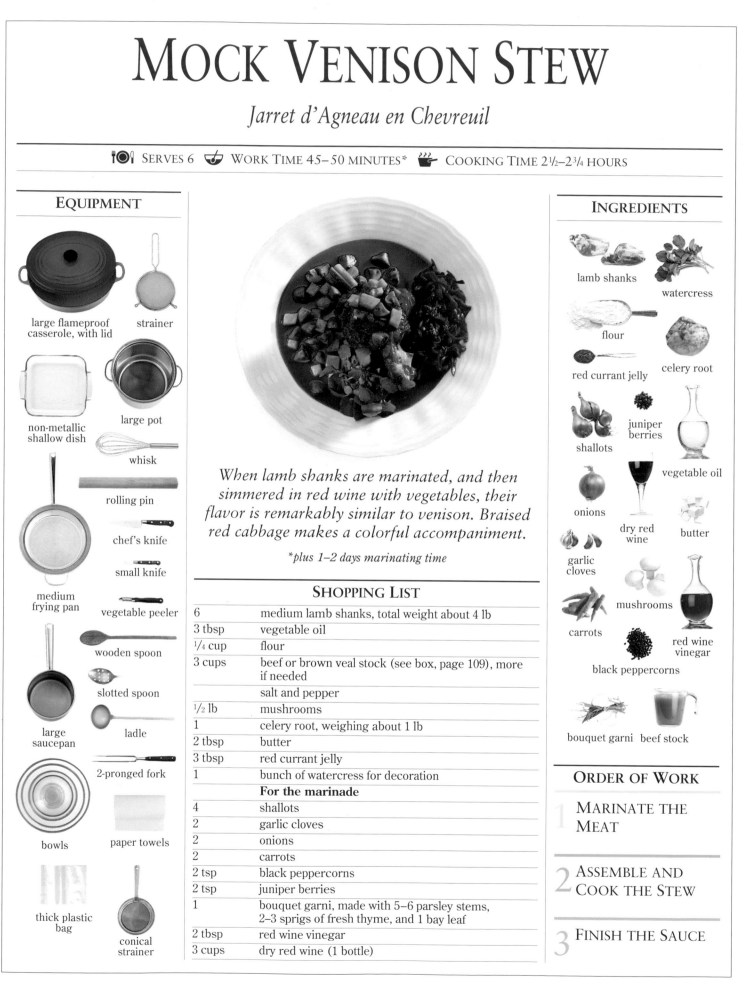

When lamb shanks are marinated, and then simmered in red wine with vegetables, their flavor is remarkably similar to venison. Braised red cabbage makes a colorful accompaniment.

*plus 1–2 days marinating time

SHOPPING LIST

6	medium lamb shanks, total weight about 4 lb
3 tbsp	vegetable oil
¼ cup	flour
3 cups	beef or brown veal stock (see box, page 109), more if needed
	salt and pepper
½ lb	mushrooms
1	celery root, weighing about 1 lb
2 tbsp	butter
3 tbsp	red currant jelly
1	bunch of watercress for decoration
	For the marinade
4	shallots
2	garlic cloves
2	onions
2	carrots
2 tsp	black peppercorns
2 tsp	juniper berries
1	bouquet garni, made with 5–6 parsley stems, 2–3 sprigs of fresh thyme, and 1 bay leaf
2 tbsp	red wine vinegar
3 cups	dry red wine (1 bottle)

INGREDIENTS

- lamb shanks
- watercress
- flour
- celery root
- red currant jelly
- shallots
- juniper berries
- vegetable oil
- onions
- dry red wine
- butter
- garlic cloves
- mushrooms
- carrots
- red wine vinegar
- black peppercorns
- bouquet garni
- beef stock

ORDER OF WORK

1 MARINATE THE MEAT

2 ASSEMBLE AND COOK THE STEW

3 FINISH THE SAUCE

MARINATE THE MEAT

1 Peel the shallots and separate into sections, if necessary. Cut each into 2–3 pieces. Set the flat side of the chef's knife on top of each garlic clove, and strike it with your fist. Discard the skin.

Leave crushed garlic cloves whole for marinating

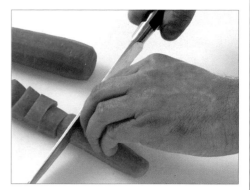

2 Peel the onions, leaving a little of the root attached, then cut them lengthwise in half. Lay each half flat on the chopping board and cut it in two.

3 Peel the carrots, using the vegetable peeler, and trim the ends, then cut them crosswise into ½-inch slices.

4 Combine the black peppercorns and juniper berries in the plastic bag. Holding the end of the bag closed, crush them using the rolling pin.

ANNE SAYS
"Crushing the peppercorns and juniper berries before adding them to the marinade releases more flavor."

Use full-bodied red wine for marinating

5 In the saucepan, combine the shallots, garlic, onions, carrots, peppercorns, juniper berries, bouquet garni, and red wine vinegar. Pour in the red wine, bring to a boil, and simmer, about 2 minutes. Transfer the marinade and vegetables to the shallow dish and set aside to cool.

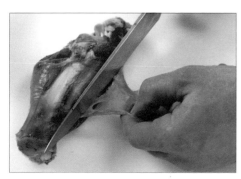

6 With the chef's knife, trim off and discard any excess fat and sinew from the lamb shanks.

7 Add the lamb shanks to the dish and stir, so they are coated with the marinade. Cover and marinate in the refrigerator, turning them occasionally, 1–2 days.

! TAKE CARE !
Make sure the marinade is cold before adding the lamb shanks, or the meat will turn sour.

2 ASSEMBLE AND COOK THE STEW

1 Heat the oven to 350°F. Transfer the lamb shanks to a plate lined with paper towels. Reserve the bouquet garni. Drain the vegetables in the strainer set over a bowl. Reserve the vegetables and marinade separately. Dry the marinated lamb shanks with paper towels.

Bouquet garni is reserved to flavor stew during cooking

2 Heat half of the oil in the casserole. Add three of the lamb shanks, and brown them well on all sides over high heat, 3–5 minutes.

3 Transfer the lamb to a bowl. Heat the remaining oil and brown the remaining shanks in the same way.

Vegetables from marinade add flavor to stew

4 Add the vegetables to the casserole and cook over medium heat, stirring frequently, until they start to brown, 5–7 minutes.

5 Sprinkle the flour over the vegetables and cook, stirring with the wooden spoon, until the flour has been absorbed and the vegetables are lightly browned, 3–5 minutes.

Bouquet garni will be
discarded at end of
cooking

Lamb will fall easily
from shank bone
when tender

6 Stir in the reserved marinade, scraping the bottom of the pan to dissolve the pan juices. Add the lamb shanks with any juices, the bouquet garni, beef stock, salt, and pepper.

ANNE SAYS
"The stock should cover the meat and vegetables so, if necessary, add more."

7 Cover, and cook in the oven, turning the lamb occasionally, until tender when pierced with the 2-pronged fork, 2–2 1/4 hours. If the sauce evaporates rapidly during cooking, add more stock. Meanwhile, prepare the mushrooms and celery root.

BEEF OR BROWN VEAL STOCK

Stock is based on raw meat bones gently simmered with aromatic vegetables in water. Boiling should be avoided because it makes the stock cloudy. Season the stock mildly so that it does not overpower the dish to which it is added.

🍽 MAKES 2–3 QUARTS

🥣 WORK TIME 20–30 MINUTES

🍲 COOKING TIME 3–4 HOURS

SHOPPING LIST

4–5 lb	beef or veal bones, cut into pieces
2	onions
2	carrots
2	celery stalks
4 quarts	water, more if needed
1	large bouquet garni
10	black peppercorns
1	garlic clove
1 tsp	tomato paste

1 Heat the oven to 450°F. Put the bones in a large roasting pan and roast until they are well browned, stirring occasionally, 30–40 minutes.

2 Peel and quarter the onions and carrots. Quarter the celery. Add the vegetables to the pan and brown, stirring occasionally, 15–20 minutes.

3 Put the vegetables and bones in a stockpot. Discard the fat from the pan, stir in 2 cups water, and bring to a boil. Add to the pot with the remaining ingredients and enough water to cover.

4 Simmer, uncovered, 4–5 hours, skimming occasionally and adding water if necessary. Strain, and boil to concentrate the flavor, if you like. Cool, and discard the fat.

8 Wipe the mushroom caps with damp paper towels and trim the stems even with the caps, using the chef's knife. Cut the mushrooms into quarters.

Cut mushrooms into quarters for attractive presentation

9 Peel the celery root. Square off the sides and cut into ½-inch slices; stack the slices and cut into ½-inch strips. Gather the strips together, and cut across into ½-inch cubes.

10 Melt the butter in the frying pan, add the celery root, and season with salt and pepper. Cook, stirring occasionally, until tender, 8–10 minutes. Transfer to a bowl.

11 Add the mushrooms to the frying pan and cook them until all the liquid has evaporated and the mushrooms are tender, 3–5 minutes. Add to the bowl with the celery root.

3 FINISH THE SAUCE

1 Using the 2-pronged fork, transfer the lamb shanks from the casserole to a plate, and reserve them.

Sauce is rich with flavor from lamb and vegetables

2 Ladle the sauce into the conical strainer set over the large pot, pressing the vegetables with the ladle to extract all the juices.

Hold conical strainer over pot while ladling in sauce and vegetables

3 Whisk the red currant jelly into the sauce with plenty of pepper. Bring the sauce back to a boil and simmer until reduced by half, 20–30 minutes.

Red currant jelly adds touch of sweetness and color to red wine sauce

Whisk constantly so red currant jelly dissolves into sauce

4 Add the mushrooms and celery root; taste for seasoning – it should be fruity, but piquant with pepper. Return the lamb to the sauce and heat until very hot, 5–10 minutes.

🍴 **TO SERVE**
Divide the stew among warmed plates; spoon over the sauce. Decorate with bouquets of watercress.

Red cabbage is a brilliant contrast to deep brown sauce

Marinated lamb shanks have distinct venison flavor

VARIATION

VENISON STEW WITH PEARS

Here, true venison is simmered with pears and red currant jelly.

1 Omit the lamb shanks. Prepare the marinade as directed. Trim the fat and sinew from 3½ lb venison stew meat and cut it into 1½-inch cubes. Marinate the meat and vegetables as directed.
2 Continue as directed, cooking the venison until tender 1¼–1½ hours.
3 Meanwhile, peel 4 firm ripe pears (total weight about 1¼ lb); cut out the flower and stem ends. Cut each pear lengthwise in half and scoop out the core. Cut each half into thirds, and put them in a bowl. Sprinkle the pears with the juice of 1 lemon, and toss to coat so they do not discolor.
4 Remove the venison from the sauce and set it aside. Strain the sauce into a large saucepan and whisk in the red currant jelly with plenty of pepper.
5 Add the pears, bring the sauce back to a boil, and simmer until tender, 6–8 minutes. Remove the pears.
6 Continue simmering the sauce until it is concentrated and has thickened slightly, 5–10 minutes. Return the venison and pears to the sauce and bring back just to a boil. Transfer the stew to a warmed tureen.

GETTING AHEAD
The cooked stew can be kept, covered, in the refrigerator, 1–2 days, or it can be frozen. Reheat it on top of the stove, and finish the sauce just before serving.

PERFECT PASTA AND CHEESE

🍽 SERVES 6　　🥄 WORK TIME 30–35 MINUTES　　🍲 BAKING TIME 25–30 MINUTES

EQUIPMENT

sauté pan

food processor

whisk

pastry brush

large pot

saucepans,
1 with lid

wooden spoon

chef's knife

2-quart soufflé
dish

small knife

nutmeg grater

cheese grater

bowls

strainer

colander

paper towels

We all relate instantly to childhood favorites like macaroni and cheese. In this grown-up version, quill-shaped pasta is baked in a simple cheese sauce, embellished with a mixture of sautéed wild and common mushrooms.

GETTING AHEAD
The complete dish can be prepared 1 day ahead and kept, covered, in the refrigerator. Bake just before serving.

SHOPPING LIST

3	shallots
3	garlic cloves
4 oz	mixed fresh wild mushrooms, such as chanterelles and shiitake
4 oz	common mushrooms
1 tbsp	butter, more for soufflé dish
	salt and pepper
³/₄ lb	quill-shaped pasta
	For the topping and cheese sauce
¹/₂ lb	sharp Cheddar cheese
1	small bunch of fresh chives
2	slices of white bread
1 quart	milk
1	slice of onion
6	black peppercorns
1	bay leaf
2 tbsp	butter
2 tbsp	flour
	freshly grated nutmeg

INGREDIENTS

quill-shaped
pasta

wild
mushrooms

Cheddar
cheese

onion

common
mushrooms

bay leaf

shallots

milk

white bread

chives

butter

flour

nutmeg †

garlic
cloves

black
peppercorns

† ground nutmeg can also be used

ANNE SAYS
"If wild are not available, use all common mushrooms."

ORDER OF WORK

1　PREPARE THE
　 MUSHROOMS

2　PREPARE THE
　 TOPPING

3　MAKE THE SAUCE;
　 FINISH THE DISH

1 PREPARE THE MUSHROOMS

1 Peel the shallots; separate into sections, if necessary. Set them flat-side down, cut them into small dice, then finely chop them.

Discard papery skins from shallots

2 Set the flat side of the chef's knife on top of each garlic clove and strike it with your fist. Discard the skin and finely chop the garlic.

3 Wipe the wild and common mushrooms with damp paper towels. Trim the stems, cutting the common mushroom stems even with the caps. Slice all the mushrooms.

2 Melt 1 tbsp butter in the sauté pan, add the shallots and sauté them, stirring, until soft, about 1 minute. Add the garlic, mushrooms, salt, and pepper. Continue cooking, stirring with the wooden spoon, until all the liquid has evaporated and the mushrooms are tender, 3–5 minutes.

ANNE SAYS
"I often buy a selection of different wild mushrooms for added flavor."

Variety of mushrooms makes dish more lively and colorful

2 PREPARE THE TOPPING

1 Grate the Cheddar cheese against the coarse grid of the grater. Coarsely chop the chives on the chopping board.

2 Discard the crusts from the bread slices and work to form coarse crumbs in the food processor. Combine with about one-quarter of the chives and 1/4 cup of the grated cheese to form the topping.

3 MAKE THE SAUCE; FINISH THE DISH

1 Scald the milk in the saucepan with the onion slice, peppercorns, and bay leaf. Remove the pan from the heat, cover, and let the milk stand in a warm place, about 10 minutes.

2 Meanwhile, melt the butter in another saucepan over medium heat. Whisk in the flour and cook until foaming, 30–60 seconds. Remove from the heat, and let cool slightly.

Freshly grated nutmeg adds aromatic flavor to sauce

3 Strain in two-thirds of the milk, and whisk to mix. Discard the onion and other flavorings. Return the pan to the heat and cook, whisking constantly, until the sauce boils and thickens.

4 Grate a little fresh nutmeg into the sauce, season with salt and pepper, and simmer the sauce, about 2 minutes longer.

Coarsely grated cheese will melt into hot sauce

5 Remove the saucepan from the heat and add the remaining grated Cheddar cheese; whisk to thoroughly combine.

6 Gradually whisk in the remaining milk. Taste the sauce for seasoning, and adjust as needed.

! TAKE CARE !
Do not reheat the sauce or the cheese will form strings.

PERFECT PASTA WITH THREE CHEESES

Spinach pasta is tossed with a rich sauce of French cheeses and baked in individual dishes.

7 Fill the large pot with water, bring to a boil, and add 1 tbsp salt. Add the quills, and simmer until they are *al dente*, 5–7 minutes, or according to package directions. Stir occasionally so they do not stick. Drain the quills in the strainer, rinse under hot water, and drain again thoroughly.

8 Heat the oven to 350°F. Butter the soufflé dish. Return the quills to the pot. Add the cheese sauce, mushrooms, and remaining chives; stir to combine. Transfer the mixture to the soufflé dish. Sprinkle with the topping. Bake until bubbling and golden brown, 25–30 minutes.

1 Omit the Cheddar cheese, shallots, mushrooms, and chives. Trim the rind from 6 oz Brie and 2 oz Roquefort cheese, then cut them into $3/8$-inch cubes. Grate 6 oz Gruyère cheese.

2 For the parsley topping: make the breadcrumbs as directed. Coarsely chop the leaves from 1 bunch of parsley. Chop 1 garlic clove. Melt 3 tbsp butter. In a bowl, combine the breadcrumbs, butter, garlic, half of the parsley, salt, and pepper.

3 Make the cheese sauce as directed, adding all of the Brie, Roquefort, and Gruyère in place of the Cheddar. Stir in 2 tsp Dijon-style mustard, and taste the sauce for seasoning, adding more mustard, if you like.

Golden breadcrumb and cheese crust tops pasta quills in a rich cheese sauce

4 Cook $1/2$ lb spinach pasta as directed. Heat the oven to 350°F. Brush 6 individual ovenproof bowls with melted butter. Drain and rinse the pasta, and return to the pot. Mix in the cheese sauce and the remaining parsley.

5 Spoon the pasta and cheese into the bowls, and sprinkle with the topping. Bake until bubbling and golden, 20–25 minutes.

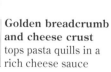

¶©¶ TO SERVE
If the top has not browned sufficiently, broil until golden, 2–3 minutes. Divide among 6 warmed plates and serve with sliced tomato salad, if you like.

Wild mushrooms with shallots and garlic update familiar pasta and cheese

BELL PEPPER AND MUSHROOM LASAGNE

†◯❙ SERVES 8   **⌣** WORK TIME 1½ HOURS   **♨** BAKING TIME 35–45 MINUTES

EQUIPMENT

- chef's knife
- ladle
- food processor †
- small knife
- wooden spoon
- slotted spoon
- large frying pan
- 2-pronged fork
- pastry brush
- bowls
- plastic bag
- 9-x13-inch baking dish
- paper towels
- large wide shallow pan
- dish towel
- large pot

† blender can also be used

A classic dish of lasagne noodles layered with ricotta cheese, mushrooms, roasted bell peppers, and tomato sauce flavored with fresh herbs. The recipe is easily doubled or tripled and freezes well.

GETTING AHEAD

The lasagne can be assembled up to 2 days ahead and kept, covered, in the refrigerator. Bake it just before serving.

SHOPPING LIST

4	red bell peppers
4	green bell peppers
1½ lb	mushrooms
2 tbsp	olive oil, more for baking dish
2 lb	ricotta cheese
1	pinch of ground nutmeg
¾ lb	lasagne noodles
1½ cups	freshly grated Parmesan cheese
	For the tomato sauce
6 lb	plum or medium tomatoes
6	garlic cloves
1	bunch of fresh basil
7–10	sprigs of fresh oregano
1	bunch of flat-leaf parsley
	salt and pepper

INGREDIENTS

- Parmesan cheese
- lasagne noodles
- olive oil
- ricotta cheese
- green bell peppers
- red bell peppers
- mushrooms
- fresh basil
- garlic cloves
- flat-leaf parsley †
- plum tomatoes ‡
- ground nutmeg
- fresh oregano

† curly parsley can also be used

‡ two 28-oz cans plum tomatoes can also be used

ORDER OF WORK

1 MAKE THE TOMATO SAUCE

2 MAKE THE FILLING AND COOK THE NOODLES

3 FINISH THE LASAGNE

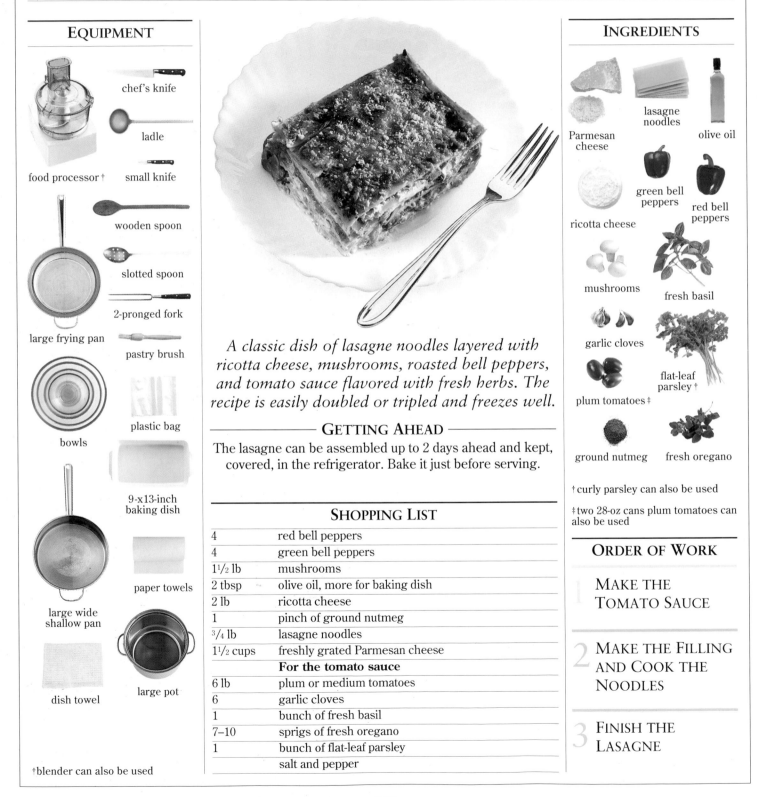

MAKE THE TOMATO SAUCE

1 Cut out the cores and score an "x" on the tomatoes. Immerse in boiling water to split the skins, 8–15 seconds. Transfer to cold water, peel, halve, and seed them; coarsely chop each half.

2 Set the flat side of the chef's knife on top of each garlic clove and strike it with your fist. Discard the skin and finely chop the garlic.

3 Strip the basil, oregano, and parsley leaves from the stems. Coarsely chop the leaves with the chef's knife.

4 Put the tomatoes, half of the garlic, and two-thirds of the chopped herbs in the shallow pan. Add salt and pepper to taste. Cook the mixture over medium heat, stirring occasionally, until slightly thickened, 25–35 minutes; there should be just a little liquid left in the pan.

Deep-red ripe tomatoes give best flavor

Basil, oregano, and flat-leaf parsley are favorite Italian herbs

5 Ladle the mixture into the food processor and purée until smooth. Taste for seasoning, and set aside.

MAKE THE FILLING AND COOK THE NOODLES

1 Roast and peel the bell peppers (see box, page 118). Cut the cores from the peppers, halve them, then scrape out the seeds.

Roasted peppers are softened and easy to slice

2 With the chef's knife, cut each roasted pepper half lengthwise into 3/8-inch strips.

Use bent fingers to guide knife

Trimmed mushrooms sit flat for slicing

3 Wipe the mushroom caps with damp paper towels, and trim the stems even with the caps. Set each of the mushrooms stem-side down on a chopping board and thinly slice them crosswise.

4 Heat the oil in the frying pan. Add the mushrooms and the remaining garlic with salt and pepper to taste, and cook, stirring occasionally, until the liquid evaporates, 10–12 minutes.

5 Put the ricotta cheese, remaining chopped herbs, the nutmeg, salt, and pepper in a medium bowl. Stir them together until thoroughly combined.

Ricotta cheese gives filling rich creamy texture

ANNE SAYS
"*If the ricotta seems dry, you can moisten it with a few spoonfuls of cream.*"

Chopped herbs are blended into filling mixture

6 Fill the large pot with water and bring to a boil. Add 1 tbsp salt and the lasagne noodles, one at a time; simmer just until tender, 8–10 minutes, or according to package directions. Using the slotted spoon, transfer the noodles to a bowl of cold water. When cool, lift them out, and drain them thoroughly on the dish towel.

HOW TO ROAST AND PEEL BELL PEPPERS

Roasting bell peppers under the broiler makes them easy to peel.

1 Heat the broiler. Set the whole bell peppers on a rack about 4 inches from the heat. Broil them, turning as needed with a 2-pronged fork, until the skins are black and blistered, 10–12 minutes.

2 Put the peppers in a plastic bag, close it, and let cool so the skins are loosened by the steam.

3 With a small knife, peel off the skins and rinse the peppers under cold running water. Pat dry with paper towels.

3 FINISH THE LASAGNE

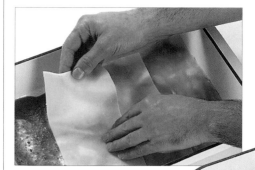

1 Heat the oven to 350°F. Brush the baking dish with oil. Spread 3–4 tbsp of the tomato sauce over the base of the dish; cover with a layer of lasagne noodles, overlapping slightly.

2 Spread one-quarter of the ricotta mixture over the noodles, then arrange one-quarter of the mushrooms and peppers on top. Spoon over about one-fifth of the remaining tomato sauce, and one-fifth of the Parmesan.

Arrange peppers evenly over mushrooms and ricotta mixture

3 Arrange a second layer of noodles on top and continue layering the lasagne ingredients until there are 4 layers, finishing with a fifth layer of noodles on top. Cover with the remaining sauce and Parmesan cheese. Bake the lasagne in the heated oven until bubbling and golden brown, 35–45 minutes.

Crisp salad
complements lasagne

¶⦿¶ TO SERVE
With the chef's knife, cut the lasagne into 8 portions, and transfer them to warmed plates. Serve with lettuce and tomato salad, if you like.

Lasagne cuts into neat portions for serving

LASAGNE WITH SPINACH

Fresh spinach is featured in this lasagne, with tomato sauce, ricotta cheese, and Parmesan cheese.

1 Make the tomato sauce as directed. Omit the bell peppers and mushrooms.
2 Discard the tough ribs and stems from 2 lb fresh spinach, then wash it thoroughly. Bring a large saucepan of salted water to a boil. Add the spinach and simmer until tender, 1–2 minutes. Drain the spinach, rinse with cold water, and drain again. Squeeze it to remove excess water, and finely chop it.
3 Peel 2 large onions, leaving a little of the root attached, halve them lengthwise, and cut them into dice.
4 Heat 3 tbsp olive oil in a large frying pan. Add the chopped onion and cook, stirring, until soft, 5–7 minutes. Add the remaining garlic, the spinach, 1 large pinch of ground nutmeg, salt, and pepper. Continue cooking, stirring occasionally, until all the liquid has evaporated, about 5 minutes. Stir in 1/2 cup heavy cream, and season to taste with salt and pepper.
5 In a medium bowl, combine the ricotta cheese, remaining herbs, a pinch of ground nutmeg, salt, and pepper.
6 Cook the noodles and assemble the lasagne as directed, layering the spinach mixture in place of the bell peppers and mushrooms. Bake the lasagne as directed; serve from the baking dish.

EGGPLANT PARMIGIANA

🍽 SERVES 8 🥄 WORK TIME 45–50 MINUTES* 🍲 BAKING TIME 40–50 MINUTES

EQUIPMENT

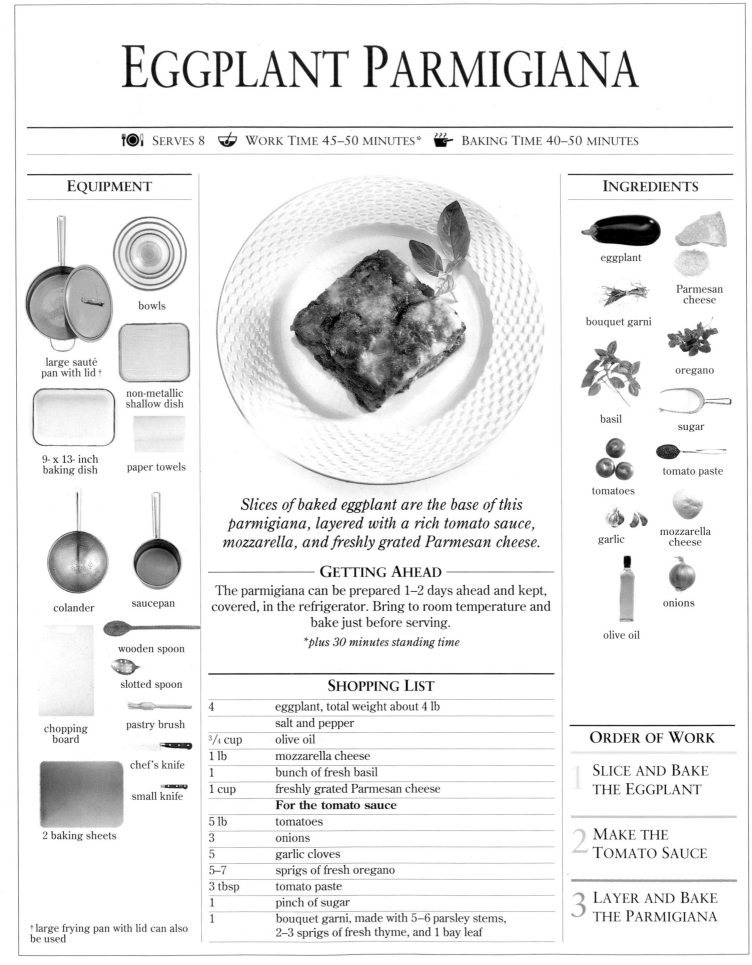

bowls

large sauté pan with lid †

non-metallic shallow dish

9- x 13- inch baking dish

paper towels

colander

saucepan

wooden spoon

slotted spoon

chopping board

pastry brush

chef's knife

small knife

2 baking sheets

† large frying pan with lid can also be used

INGREDIENTS

eggplant

Parmesan cheese

bouquet garni

oregano

basil

sugar

tomatoes

tomato paste

garlic

mozzarella cheese

olive oil

onions

Slices of baked eggplant are the base of this parmigiana, layered with a rich tomato sauce, mozzarella, and freshly grated Parmesan cheese.

GETTING AHEAD
The parmigiana can be prepared 1–2 days ahead and kept, covered, in the refrigerator. Bring to room temperature and bake just before serving.

*plus 30 minutes standing time

SHOPPING LIST

4	eggplant, total weight about 4 lb
	salt and pepper
³/₄ cup	olive oil
1 lb	mozzarella cheese
1	bunch of fresh basil
1 cup	freshly grated Parmesan cheese
	For the tomato sauce
5 lb	tomatoes
3	onions
5	garlic cloves
5–7	sprigs of fresh oregano
3 tbsp	tomato paste
1	pinch of sugar
1	bouquet garni, made with 5–6 parsley stems, 2–3 sprigs of fresh thyme, and 1 bay leaf

ORDER OF WORK

1 SLICE AND BAKE THE EGGPLANT

2 MAKE THE TOMATO SAUCE

3 LAYER AND BAKE THE PARMIGIANA

1 SLICE AND BAKE THE EGGPLANT

1 Trim the stem ends from each of the eggplant and cut them crosswise into ¹/₂-inch slices, using the chef's knife.

Good eggplant are firm and shiny with no brown patches

2 Lay the slices in the shallow dish and sprinkle with salt; let stand to draw out the bitter juices, 30 minutes.

3 Heat the oven to 350°F. Transfer the eggplant slices to the colander and rinse them well under cold running water to remove the salt. Dry the slices thoroughly on paper towels.

4 Oil the baking sheets. Lay the eggplant slices on the sheets, and brush with oil. Bake just until tender, turning once and brushing again with oil, 20–25 minutes. Meanwhile, make the tomato sauce.

2 MAKE THE TOMATO SAUCE

Skin from crushed garlic comes off easily in your fingers

1 Cut the cores from the tomatoes and score an "x" on the base of each. Immerse in boiling water until the skins start to split, 8–15 seconds. Transfer at once to cold water. When cool, peel off the skins. Cut them crosswise in half, squeeze out the seeds, then coarsely chop each half.

2 Peel the onions, leaving a little of the root attached, then cut them lengthwise in half. Lay each half cut-side down and slice horizontally, then vertically, toward the root, leaving the slices attached at the root end. Finally, cut across the onion half to make dice, and chop until very fine.

3 Set the flat side of the chef's knife on top of each garlic clove, and strike it with your fist. Discard the skin, and finely chop the garlic.

4 Strip the oregano leaves from the stems and pile the leaves on the chopping board. With the chef's knife, coarsely chop the leaves.

5 Heat the remaining oil in the sauté pan, add the onions, and cook over medium heat, stirring occasionally with the wooden spoon, until soft but not brown, 3–4 minutes.

Sautéed onions form base of tomato sauce

Tomatoes will cook to moist pulp in sauce so need only be roughly chopped

6 Add the chopped tomatoes to the sauté pan with the garlic, oregano, tomato paste, salt, pepper, sugar, and bouquet garni; stir to combine.

7 Cover the sauté pan, and simmer the sauce over very low heat, 15 minutes. Uncover and continue cooking, stirring occasionally, until thick, about 15 minutes longer. Discard the bouquet garni and taste for seasoning.

ANNE SAYS
"The small amount of sugar in the sauce helps cut the acidity in tomatoes."

3 LAYER AND BAKE THE PARMIGIANA

Mozzarella cubes will melt as parmigiana cooks

1 Cut the mozzarella into ¹/₂-inch slices. Stack the slices and cut into ¹/₂-inch strips. Gather the strips together and cut into cubes. Strip the basil leaves from the stems, reserving 8 sprigs for garnish. Stack the leaves, roll up tightly, and finely shred.

2 Spread about one-quarter of the tomato sauce over the bottom of the baking dish. Arrange one-third of the eggplant slices on top of the sauce in rows, overlapping them slightly.

3 Cover the eggplant slices with about one-third of the shredded basil leaves, one-quarter of the grated Parmesan cheese, and one-quarter of the mozzarella cubes.

Sprinkle mozzarella cheese evenly over eggplant slices

4 Repeat layering the tomato sauce, eggplant slices, basil, Parmesan, and mozzarella to form 3 layers. Top with the remaining tomato sauce, mozzarella, and Parmesan. Bake in the oven until bubbling and lightly browned on top, 20–25 minutes. Leave the dish to stand, 15 minutes.

TO SERVE
Cut the parmigiana into 8 portions, and serve on warmed plates.

Parmesan and mozzarella cheese enrich parmigiana

Basil sprig makes attractive decoration

TIAN OF MEDITERRANEAN VEGETABLES

In Provence, vegetables are often baked in a traditional tian *or earthenware dish.*

1 Omit the tomato sauce and mozzarella. Trim and slice 6 small eggplant (total weight about 2 lb) and 3 large zucchini (total weight about 1½ lb). Salt the eggplant and zucchini slices and rinse as directed.
2 Slice 6 large onions into thin rings. Heat 2 tbsp olive oil in a large sauté pan; add the onions, salt, and pepper. Cover with foil and cook over low heat, stirring occasionally, until soft and starting to brown, 20–25 minutes.
3 Peel, seed, and chop 3 lb tomatoes. Strip the leaves from 1 bunch of fresh thyme. Add the tomatoes and three-quarters of the thyme leaves to the pan; cook, uncovered, as directed, about 10 minutes longer.
4 Brush eight 6-inch gratin dishes with oil. Spread most of the tomato mixture in each dish, reserving about ½ cup. Cover with the eggplant and zucchini, alternating in a spiral pattern.
5 Sprinkle each dish with 1 tsp olive oil, the remaining thyme, salt, and pepper. Bake, 15–20 minutes. Add a spoonful of the reserved tomato mixture to the center of each dish. Sprinkle with an additional 1 tsp oil and 1 tbsp Parmesan cheese; continue baking until tender when pierced with a knife, 10–15 minutes longer.

CASSEROLES KNOW-HOW

A casserole, piping hot and straight from the oven, embodies the notion of home cooking. Whether you are serving an informal supper, or a large crowd, always use the freshest ingredients.

CHOOSING CASSEROLES

Occasion and audience are the first questions to ask when choosing a casserole. For a relaxed buffet or a party, recipes like Paella, Bell Pepper and Mushroom Lasagne, or Beef, Barley, and Mushroom Stew form a complete meal and are easy to serve in large quantities. The season should be taken into account, with Old Emily's Shepherd's Pie or Chicken and Beer Stew inviting in cold weather. In summer plenty of vegetables and fish are appropriate, as in Seafood and Tomato Stew or Tian of Mediterranean Vegetables. Sophisticated dishes like Five-Spice Fillet of Salmon and Tarragon Chicken would grace the grandest dinner.

GETTING AHEAD WITH CASSEROLES

A great advantage of casseroles is that they can frequently be prepared, assembled, and even cooked in advance. Many actually improve, like Turkey Mole or Shrimp and Okra Gumbo. Recipes that are baked before serving, such as Eggplant Parmigiana, are ideal for preparing in advance, because all the work can be done ahead, with only the baking to be done at the last minute. Most dishes in sauce can be reheated, either in a moderate oven or on top of the stove. However, beware of sauces that can separate – cream, butter, or eggs are best added at the last minute.

Reheat using low heat to warm the food evenly and give the best results. Personally I prefer to reheat dishes in the oven, because they are less likely to scorch on the bottom of the pan. Note that flour-based sauces often thicken when they are left to stand, so they may have to be thinned with whatever liquid is appropriate.

FISH STOCK

🍽 MAKES ABOUT 1 QUART

🥣 WORK TIME 10–15 MINUTES

🍲 COOKING TIME 20 MINUTES

SHOPPING LIST

1 lb	fish bones and heads, cut into 2-inch pieces
1	onion, thinly sliced
1 cup	dry white wine
1 quart	water
3–5	sprigs of parsley
1 tsp	peppercorns

1 Wash the fish bones and heads; place them in a medium saucepan with the remaining ingredients.

2 Bring to a boil, and simmer, skimming occasionally with a large metal spoon, 20 minutes.

3 Strain the stock into a bowl. Cool, then cover, and keep in the refrigerator.

WHITE VEAL STOCK

🍽 MAKES ABOUT 2–3 QUARTS

🥣 WORK TIME 20–30 MINUTES

🍲 COOKING TIME 4–5 HOURS

SHOPPING LIST

4–5 lb	veal bones, cut into pieces
4 quarts	water, more for blanching
2	onions, quartered
2	carrots, quartered
2	celery stalks, quartered
10	peppercorns
1	bouquet garni
1	garlic clove

1 Put the veal bones in a large pot and cover with water. Simmer, 5 minutes, drain, and rinse well.

2 Return the bones to the pot with the remaining ingredients. Bring to a boil, skimming often, and simmer, 4–5 hours, skimming occasionally.

3 Strain the stock, and boil to concentrate the flavor, if you like. Cool, then cover, and keep in the refrigerator.

CASSEROLES AND YOUR HEALTH

By combining proteins, vegetables, and grains, casseroles help to balance your diet. If calories, cholesterol, and fat need to be considered, some casseroles can be easily modified to suit your needs. Many casseroles are either simmered or baked, so a minimum of fat is added during the cooking process. Some recipes are naturally low in fat. In others, the quantity of fat can be reduced or omitted altogether. When frying or sautéing, you can use olive oil or vegetable oil in place of butter. To keep cholesterol in check, the amount of meat, chicken, or fish can be reduced, and the quantity of vegetables increased. Omit rich ingredients, such as bacon, heavy cream, and sour cream. All-vegetable recipes, like Eggplant Parmigiana, Bell Pepper and Mushroom Lasagne, and Perfect Pasta and Cheese, accompanied by a green salad, make a substantial vegetarian main course offering.

MICROWAVE COOKING

A microwave oven can be used to speed up the preparation of some ingredients. For example, it can help with the peeling of shallots and onions. To peel 3 oz small onions or shallots, trim them and heat them in a microwave-safe bowl on High (100% power), 45 seconds. Squeeze each stalk end until the onion or shallot pops out of its skin. For tear-free onion chopping or slicing, trim the ends off the onion, then place the onion on paper towels on the microwave oven floor, and heat on High (100% power), 1 minute. Remove the skin, then slice or chop as desired.

PRESENTING CASSEROLES

I suggest many ways to present all these casseroles attractively, perhaps with garnishes of colorful herbs or twists of lemon. Some dishes are browned in the oven, a decoration in itself. A wealth of cooking dishes are available to go in the oven and take to the table, or you may prefer to transfer the food to a fresh serving dish after cooking, remembering that many have broth or a sauce and may therefore require a deep bowl. A ladle is often the appropriate serving utensil.

Many casseroles need no accompaniment and come complete with kidney beans, rice, barley, or some other carbohydrate. They may have a topping of mashed potato like French Meat and Herb Potato Pie or may be layered with pasta, like Lasagne with Spinach. Others may need an accompaniment to balance spicy flavors or a rich sauce. Unusual grains like couscous or buckwheat are a popular choice. It is hard to go wrong with a side dish of mashed potatoes, or boiled new potatoes in their skins. And simplest of all is a loaf of crusty brown or sourdough bread.

HOW-TO BOXES

In each **Creative Casseroles** *recipe you'll find pictures of all the techniques used. Some basic preparations appear in a number of recipes; these are shown in detail in "how-to" boxes:*

INDEX

ACKNOWLEDGMENTS

Photographers David Murray
Jules Selmes
Photographer's Assistant Steve Head

Chef Eric Treuille
Cookery Consultant Martha Holmberg
Home Economist Sarah Lowman

US Editor Jeanette Mall

Typesetting Linda Parker
Text film by Disc to Print (UK) Limited

Production Consultant Lorraine Baird

*Anne Willan would like to thank her chief
editor Hilaire Walden, associate editor
Jackie Bobrow, and consultant editor
Cynthia Nims for their vital help with
writing this book and researching and
testing the recipes, aided by Joanna Rend
and Jane Reilly with La Varenne's chefs
and trainees.*